Voices on the Family

Compiled by Marilynne E. Foster

Christian Publications

CAMP HILL, PENNSYLVANIA

ꭵ Christian Publications

3825 Hartzdale Drive, Camp Hill, PA 17011
www.cpi-horizon.com
www.christianpublications.com

Faithful, biblical publishing since 1883

Voices on the Family
ISBN: 0-87509-926-2
LOC Control Number: 2001-130442

© 2001 by Christian Publications, Inc.

01 02 03 04 05   5 4 3 2 1

Contents

Foreword v

On Being a Family

1. Friendship Close to Home/
   Cheryl Smith 3
2. What Would They Do without Me?/
   Lola Gillebaard 21
3. No Good Thing . . ./
   William Cutts 27
4. Baboo/
   Marie Ens 31
5. When a Father Abandons His Children/
   Ron Ballard 35
6. Widow with a Husband/
   Corinne Sahlberg 49

Under the Same Roof

7. Teaching a Skill/
   Michael Phillips 63
8. Busy Hands Are Franctic Hands/
   Sheila Rabe 93
9. Values That Form Us/
   Mark Lee 103
10. Speaking Childese—Fathers and Communication/
    Michael Phillips 129

When the Times Get Tough

11. Contemplating Widowhood/
    Arlene Peters 159

12. Hope for Hurting Parents—
    When Grown Children Make Bad Choices/
    Tom Allen 165

13. The Widow's Might/
    Marie Ens 183

14. Backyard War/
    Jim and Jean Livingston 189

15. Wonderful Complications/
    Martin St. Kilda 201

16. Yong's Last Gift/
    Marie Ens 213

17. A Promise Kept/
    Ruth Presswood Hutchins 219

Seasons of Life

18. Memories: Dealing with Reminders/
    Welby O'Brien 233

19. My Turn/
    Rosalie Flickinger 243

20. Who's the Child?/
    Sheila Rabe 251

21. The Way of a Widow/
    Marie Ens 263

22. Monster from the Deep/
    Robert Bell and Bruce Lockerbie 267

23. Grandmothering: The Great Frontier/
    Sheila Rabe 279

24. Chivalry—The Lost Virtue/
    Steve Masterson with George McPeek 287

25. Make Good Memories Now/
    William R. Goetz 293

Foreword

Our lives are filled with discussions about issues that have enormous implications: our nation's economy, the war on drugs, international terrorism, world hunger, AIDS and the environment, to mention a few.

To those of us who are believers in the sovereign God who loves this sin-cursed world in which we live, there are even more important and compelling issues. We're concerned about lost people. We want to see the gospel preached across the world. We are passionate about lifting up the glory of God.

But as we watch our nation pursue the illusive dream of the good life and even as we evaluate our own life experience, we come to one inescapable conclusion. The institution of the family as ordained by God, where He is exalted, children are loved and the marriage covenant is honored, is a fundamental building block of every society. To suppose that we as Christians can be successful in Great Commission work, while failing to nurture our own marriages and mentor our own children, is to deny the clear teaching of Scripture.

Because we have not always caught the reality of this truth, *Voices on the Family* is a welcome addition to the *Voices* series. It is a collection of impressive, often moving, essays and biographical sketches that allow us to see people in the throes of challenging life situations. Some of the chapters deal with issues of communication, others with sorrow and death. There is a story about grandmothering and another about godly parents whose children live their lives in a spirit of rebellion. These are real stories about real people sharing real experiences.

While family issues are central to this book, the authors do not suggest that our responsibility to serve God wholeheartedly must be sacrificed on the altar of the family. There is an appropriate balance to be achieved, and this book gives us a better understanding of how this goal can be more fully realized.

Dr. Peter N. Nanfelt, President
The Christian and Missionary Alliance

On Being a Family

Friendship Close to Home

taken from
Kindling a Kindred Spirit

by Cheryl Smith

With red, puffy eyes and a quivering lower lip, Sierra stood before me bemoaning her fate.

"It's an honor to be chosen to play Mary in the Christmas program," I explained patiently. "All you have to do is sit up there and look holy. You'll do fine."

"But I don't want to be Mary! At first I said I'd do it, but now I've changed my mind," Sierra protested.

"Why would it be so awful?" I inquired further, a bit exasperated.

"Someone said, 'I'm sure glad I don't have to be Mary. Daniel's *ugly!*' And now I have to stand next to him as Mary." Then, assured that she was on the path to public humiliation, Sierra again burst into a flood of tears.

I did my best to stifle a smile and wondered how a lanky, freckled third-grade boy could ever appear ugly.

"Who told you that?" I probed.

"His sister!" Sierra reported with emphasis.

"Well, what would you expect from a sister? I sincerely doubt Daniel is ugly. But I suppose the original Mary may have had some of the same misgivings about her Joseph that you are having. The difference is that for her, the arrangement was permanent, and she probably had no say." Then I shared a similar experience when I was Mary in a Christmas pageant appearing opposite a Joseph I wasn't too sure of either.

"How did you feel?" Sierra sniffed, as she contemplated the possibility that her mother had survived such a fate.

"I recall feeling much the way you did. I was very nervous, but also a little excited. The boy picked for Joseph was pretty wild, but I also thought he was kinda cute."

Somehow that amazing confession filled Sierra with the strength to later don her sheets, pick up her baby doll and fulfill her role as Mary in the annual Christmas pageant. Daniel, clad in a bathrobe, dutifully knelt beside her—close enough to be considered a couple, but just barely.

A History of Marital Friendship

Perhaps Sierra and Daniel weren't that unlike the original Mary and Joseph. We know that Joseph was compassionate toward Mary. When he learned that Mary was pregnant, he planned to divorce her privately rather than make the divorce a public spectacle. But the blend of compassion and faith we see in the introductory remarks in Matthew and Luke hardly describe a deep, abiding friendship. The truth is that most marriages throughout history were rather passionless. Prior to Christ, women were largely viewed in subservient positions. Marriages were arranged for financial or political gain, for producing heirs to preserve the family line and for managing a man's estate. Friendship between husband and wife might eventually characterize a marriage, but it certainly wasn't expected. Instead, couples fell into their prescribed social roles and the cycle of birth, life and death rolled onward. It was only as a result of the teachings of Christ that the wife was elevated to full, equal standing with her husband. That was why it was necessary for Paul to admonish the Christian wife to submit to her husband, and for a Christian husband to love his wife actively (see Ephesians 5). The way Christian couples treated each other was evidence of their conversion. These were radically new social concepts.

Through the cross, men and women have equal worth (see Galatians 3:28). It may be hard for us to appreciate the radical impact of this message, but it was truly revolutionary. In Jesus' day, for example, divorce was a singularly male privilege. A husband could legally dismiss his wife for any reason, and she had no recourse.

The role of women has changed dramatically over the years. With the advent of the twentieth century, new options were offered to Western women. In 1919 women earned the right to vote. As a result of World Wars I and II, women were thrust from the home into the workplace where they earned respect as providers. Educational opportunities followed. Today few professions are without female employees.

In addition, the average lifespan has been extended. In the old days, few had the time to waste on extramarital affairs much less midlife crises. Indeed, it is only with the modern era that many of the relational issues facing marriages have arisen.

These changes have made it necessary for couples to attend seriously to their marriages. No longer is marriage an inviolate contract held together by social pressure. The result for many is that marriage has become a choice regulated by the quality of the marriage relationship.

Why Lovers Need to Be Friends

Reason #1: Friendship Protects Marriages

We all know that adultery is wrong. Many spouses can't imagine themselves ever being wooed away by another. "That would never happen to us," Kay says confidently. "Besides, we are committed to each another. I know Joe would never think of fooling around." But her confidence may be ungrounded if she and Joe are not investing in the friendship their marriage offers. It certainly is ungrounded if their primary emotional investments are being made elsewhere.

While we may be quick to condemn adultery, many people see no harm in building their closest friendships outside of their marriages. The early disillusionments of married life often convince a spouse that her chosen mate is incapable of becoming her best friend. For example, a friend at work may seem to understand these feelings. She may share the same interests, values and concerns. Often it is all too easy to begin making the emotional investments in the friendship like this alone. Perhaps her mate has chosen to do the same. Neglected, the marriage relationship withers. What started out as a passionate promise with the highest of hopes becomes routine and lifeless. They talk less. They spend less time together. Before long, the marriage resembles little more than a roommate arrangement. Intimacy has died. And because society no longer honors marriage as a lifetime commitment, divorce seems an acceptable solution.

But divorce need not be the only solution for a dying relationship. Instead, nurture your marriage into a warm, committed friendship. Such a relationship is not only a rich blessing, but is also the greatest protection from the undermining attitudes and temptations of the world. As one author wrote, "Marriages usually don't collapse overnight. They become bankrupt gradually because they lack daily deposits of love, communication, and affirmation."[1] Every couple needs to realize that nurturing their marriage friendship is an insurance policy they can't do without.

Reason #2: Friendship Is God's Plan for Marriage

God's plan for marriage is another reason marriage needs to evolve into friendship. Adam's aloneness was the only aspect of God's creation deemed incomplete. Thus, Eve was lovingly created to meet Adam's relational needs (see Genesis 2:18). But their marriage amounted to more than Eve's role versus Adam's. In fact, neither Adam nor Eve even thought about who should take out the trash, mow the lawn or do the dishes. Roles were irrelevant before they sinned. Instead, unity was the object of their relationship.

As the first couple came together they surrendered their separate identities to discover a union made of their strengths, weaknesses, likes and dislikes. Adam and Eve became a team. Their mission was to rule the world. It wasn't until Adam and Eve were disobedient that it was necessary to designate roles in marriage. Cooperation, not competition, reigns where perfect love exists. In the beginning, Adam and Eve's bond of friendship ruled their hearts making role definitions unnecessary.

Today wives need to be reminded to love and respect their husbands. Husbands need to be reminded to care lovingly for their wives. A growing friendship and individual roles for the husband and wife remain part of God's plan for marriage. Unlike roles, however, friendship cannot be commanded into existence. God leaves the nurturing of such a dimension to us.

Reason #3: Friendship Leads to Maturity

Someone wrote: "Romance talks about love; friendship puts it to the ultimate test."[2] How true! It's one thing to be stirred emotionally by dreams of marital bliss prior to marriage and something else to live with the differences married life soon uncovers. After all, how were you to know that your mate would insist on sleeping with the windows wide open or that his idea of hanging up clothes was a heap in the corner of the bedroom? How was he supposed to know that when you were upset, you needed a soft hug and listening ear but *not* solutions? Indeed, the differences married life reveals can seem so great that many couples wonder how they ever got together in the first place. This is where friendship can make or break the relationship. The decision must be made either to adapt to one another and work things through or to wallow in disillusionment and make emotional investments elsewhere.

In this way the adjustments of marriage give a unique opportunity to mature. After all, few best friends could endure living together. In spite of their warm compatibility, their differences would eventually drive them apart. Only a marriage bound by a solid promise of loyalty before God and one another can carry two people through this difficult maturing process. Marriage offers the opportunity to develop elements of character (patience, self-control, long-suffering, loyalty) which are left undeveloped by less demanding friendships. Granted, the life-shaping conflicts of marriage are far from comfortable, but worked through in God's strength, such conflicts offer a sure path to maturity.

Reason #4: Friendship Expands Your Horizons

Do you remember the Greek myth about Narcissus? He was such an arrogant, self-absorbed youth that he spurned all offers of love. Then one day he sat down to rest at the edge of a spring and caught his reflection in the water. He was so enthralled with the beauty of his own image that he was unable to leave. Instead, he sat there gazing into the pool until he wasted away into the flower that now bears his name.

The moral seems as clear as Narcissus' reflection: Self-absorption stunts the personality and ultimately destroys it. None of us is strong enough to live as an island. What God said for Adam applies to all mankind: "It is not good for the man to be alone" (Genesis 2:18). Friendship helps to provide balance in life and saves us from undue introspection.

Narcissus had a friend whose name was Echo. Echo was a nymph who was only able to parrot what another said. It was a comfortable relationship because it made for few differences. Then one day she followed Narcissus on a hunting trip into the mountains. When he fell into trouble, Narcissus called for help. Echo answered but was unable to give him the counsel he needed. In the end, Narcissus forsook Echo. Heartbroken, Echo stayed in the mountains mourning for Narcissus until only her voice was left.

It is our differences that make marital friendship both a challenge and rare blessing. He was raised in suburbia. She grew up in the country. He was a firstborn child in a family of four. She was the third in a family of six. His parents were Catholic. She never went to church until high school. He likes to camp and fish. She likes to shop.

These are just some of the differences marriage uncovers. When the fires of initial romance have cooled, rediscovering common ground can prove to be challenging. Instead of drawing us into new experiences, we often allow differences like these to repel us. It is easy to see how common interests build quick friendships. There is nothing wrong with having friends who enjoy the same things you do. But friendships based on commonality alone lack opportunities for growth. The world is full of enriching new experiences and perspectives to be embraced with an adventurous, open spirit. Many of these experiences are possible through the differences between spouses. The trick is to make such differences bridges instead of barriers.

My husband took me golfing on our honeymoon. After several frustrating holes and countless minutes in the weeds searching for my ball, I very dramatically threw down my club, burst into tears and announced that I would never play this "stupid" game again. I haven't, either. But I have learned to caddy. Walking with my husband over a manicured course, I've come to appreciate the landscaping and the expertise that golfing requires. You might find this hard to believe, but sometimes I'll even watch a little golf on TV. I still have no desire to golf and I'm sure course owners are relieved by the news. But this is just one example of how we were able to make a difference into a bridge instead of a barrier. Whatever your differences, you can do the same. Provided your mate's interests are not sinful, you too can compromise to expand your horizons. You'll be richer for doing so.

Are the differences between you and your spouse becoming barriers? Are you tempted to dream of a mate more like yourself? Ask God to give you a new perspective because the differences in a loving friendship can enrich and broaden life. As the ancient Greek myth of Echo and Narcissus illustrates, we need other perspectives to guide and improve our lives.

While books and seminars on improving marriage abound, comparatively little attention is given to the friendship aspect of marriage. Yet friendship with a spouse affects every aspect of the relationship. As two professional counselors noted: "Love, in the absence of friendship, is only a hormonal illusion. One cannot desire another person over the long haul without really being friends with him or her."[3] It is friendship that gives enduring strength and warmth to marriage.

The concept of befriending a mate may appear impossible. How long has it been since you've done something special together? Friendships are built on investments of time that turn into treasured memories. In his helpful book, *Creative Romance*, Doug Fields shares his philosophy for marital dating: "My wife and I are sure to have disappointing episodes and some regretful moments. But one of our goals is to make sure that our positive memories outweigh our heartaches."[4] What a great goal! But the mental photo albums of many couples hold only bitter recollections. After collecting a few pages of such experiences, they give up or begin building positive memories with others. But it is possible to transform many disappointments into fun memories.

Making Memories

I remember one couple recounting their first camping trip. The retelling of the disastrous weekend was so funny we laughed until we cried. True, they never became veteran campers, but they had succeeded in turning a bitter experience into a fun memory. How we view life ultimately boils down to a matter of perspective. Satan's perspective is always a shrinking, bitter, pessimistic outlook. The perspective of faith trusts God to heal the past and bring a brighter tomorrow.

The reason some couples quit dating is that they seem to have less and less to talk about. The awkward silence between them is uncomfortable. Many times, it seems easier to stay apart than face the emotional reality of their dying relationship. If this resembles your situation, start by doing something small together. Watch sports on TV, go to a movie or concert or do something with your children or another couple. Stay away from situations that require sustained conversation or deteriorate into undue introspection. Instead start small, and try not to expect too much too soon.

If you are in a relationship where you have little to say to one another, intimacy has virtually died. You really need to begin afresh to build your marital friendship. Provide simple, nonthreatening memories at the beginning. As you rediscover one another, you can move on to planning bigger experiences together.

Probably one of the biggest blockades to marital dating is that couples don't enjoy doing the same things. Before you were married you both wanted to impress each other with how loving and flexible you were. After a few years of marriage, you may be sick of "going along" and are ready to reveal that you despise fishing, shopping or whatever.

Having your own interests isn't wrong. Couples who are best friends don't necessarily do everything together. The challenge is to discover new interests that both can share such as the kids' sporting events or a new hobby. Suddenly your interests broaden and you've found a way to build another memory.

Practice Forgiving

Forgiveness is difficult because it is so costly. Someone must bear the consequences for the wrong that has taken place. Christ bore the pain of our sin when He died on the cross. If Jesus wanted revenge, He would now be making us suffer for the pain our sin caused Him. Instead, Jesus drew on God's grace to bear the sting of sin and extended to us His unreserved love and forgiveness. Without His attitude of grace, friendship with Christ would be impossible.

Paul said this is the same attitude we are to imitate when approaching earthly relationships. It is impossible to do on our own. None of us can extend the same forgiveness that Christ did. Such attitudes are foreign to our self-centered nature. Yet when we allow God to change our hearts, He has promised to help us treat one another with the attitudes that build rather than destroy.

Tracy and Martin had been married for nine years. They hadn't been easy years either. Financial stress was a constant burden. Even after advanced training and several job changes, Martin's career still seemed headed nowhere. With three small children underfoot, Tracy began to long for some sense of permanence and security in their lives. What began as willing sacrifices on her part faded into a bitter cycle of high hopes and disappointments.

Tracy's disillusionment fueled Martin's frustration. When she tried to express her feelings, he felt accused by her unhappiness. She, in turn, felt neglected, unappreciated and misunderstood. Conversation between them dribbled to a near standstill. Increasingly, they spent their time in different worlds. Tracy was involved with the children. Martin was lost in his work. Although both were Christians, Tracy finally had to face the bleak future of her marriage if something didn't change.

"I don't know how much longer I can stand it," she confided to a friend. "I don't love him anymore. We argue all the time. If the right guy came along and showed some interest in me, I know I'd leave."

Like many, Martin and Tracy's marriage might easily have ended in divorce. Instead Tracy allowed the Holy Spirit to make a difference. She realized she couldn't change Martin. But she could allow God to change her, and that's where she began. This decision was a significant step in saving her marriage.

Martin and Tracy survived the disillusionments of marriage because they focused first on Christ. Through His Word and godly counsel they were able to change their attitudes and, in turn, heal their marriage. Today Martin and Tracy enjoy a close friendship and are together confronting the joys and hardships life presents.

Working through past hurts to renew a relationship is tough, complicated work. However, we serve an all-powerful God who wants your marriage not only to succeed, but also to blossom into friendship. Don't give up before you give Him a chance.

Actions Speak Louder than Words

Wedged between two immense volumes of Jewish history, the small book of Ruth holds a tender picture of marital friendship. Ruth met and married her first husband in her native land of Moab. After his death, she left Moab to live in Judah with her mother-in-law. Both widowed, they settled in Bethlehem, and Ruth soon began working as a gleaner in the fields.

Gleaners would walk behind the reapers to collect any grain that was dropped. Portions of the field were also left for the gleaners to harvest. This practice was outlined in the Law as God's provision for the needy, especially widows (see Leviticus 19:9-10). However, having the legal right to reap was where the gleaner's protection ended. The Law didn't specify how much should be left for the needy. No doubt, many owners made it difficult for the gleaners to collect a day's wage. It is certain that they were often the targets of verbal and sometimes physical abuse.

God guided Ruth to Boaz's field. When Boaz arrived at the field, he noticed Ruth and asked one of the servants about her. "She is the Moabitess who came back from Moab with Naomi," the servant replied. "She went into the field and has worked steadily from morning till now, except for a short rest in the shelter" (Ruth 2:6-7).

Next, Boaz addresses Ruth personally. "My daughter, listen to me," he says kindly.

> Don't go and glean in another field and don't go away from here. Stay here with my servant girls. Watch the field where the men are harvesting, and follow along after the girls. I have told the men not to touch you. And whenever you are thirsty, go and get a drink from the water jars the men have filled. (2:8-9)

In these few words, Boaz demonstrated extraordinary kindness to Ruth. What a comfort on the first day of gleaning, that Boaz, an esteemed landowner in Bethlehem, offered his welcome and protection to her. She was also invited to drink from the water supply whenever she needed to. This may not seem like a big kindness to us, but in a hot land where water was scarce and had to be drawn by hand, access to drinking water was a privilege.

Boaz's kindness overwhelmed Ruth. Bowing down before him, she asked the obvious question: "Why have I found such favor in your eyes that you notice me—a foreigner?" (2:10).

Boaz responded, "I've been told all about what you have done for your mother-in-law since the death of your husband" (2:11). Then he gave Ruth a special blessing:

"May the LORD repay you for what you have done. May you be richly rewarded by the LORD, the God of Israel, under whose wings you have come to take refuge" (2:12).

If only everyone could hear such encouragement on his or her first day of work! Ruth could hardly believe it herself. "May I continue to find favor in your eyes, my lord," she said to Boaz. "You have given me comfort and have spoken kindly to your servant—though I do not have the standing of one of your servant girls" (2:13).

But Boaz wasn't finished. Later he invited her to join his harvest crew in a meal. Boaz even served her personally. When she returned to work, Boaz instructed the harvesters to leave extra grain for her and prohibited them from embarrassing her in any way.

Is it any wonder that Ruth stayed in Boaz's field the rest of the harvest season? Is it any wonder that she later asked him to marry her? Boaz was much older. Even by his own words, he didn't consider himself a desirable mate for young Ruth (3:10). Yet after watching Boaz and receiving his kindnesses day after day, Ruth was ready to risk the misunderstanding her forwardness might produce.

So often we think of big, dramatic gifts when we think of demonstrating our love—a dozen roses, a romantic dinner in a fine restaurant, an expensive vacation, etc. But it is really the little daily gestures that keep a friendship alive, things like compliments or helping out when you can. It's a touch that communicates comfort or esteem. Kindness includes making time together a priority, rather than giving your spouse the leftovers of your day. It is going that little bit extra when it's unexpected. Surprise dates and gifts can be fun, but the warmth of a friendship is largely built on the multitude of the little considerate acts sown throughout the years.

Words Have Power Too

Words have incredible power to build or destroy. Through our conversation, we can bring out the best or worst in one another. It's no surprise that Paul mentions conversation in his passage on relationships in Ephesians. He wrote: "Do not let any unwholesome talk come out of your mouths, but only what is helpful for building others up according to their needs, that it may benefit those who listen" (Ephesians 4:29). Everyone needs to memorize and apply this counsel. For if we only spoke what was helpful, needful and timely, we could avoid many heartaches.

Reading through the Song of Songs recently, I was struck not as much by the poetry but by the power of words. The romantic couple is intent on building their love. Everything they say to one another drips with passion. Then one evening the husband comes home late only to find the door locked. Knocking at the door, he begs her to let him in. This time she is a bit put out. It is late. She's already in bed and could care less about Prince Charming's predicament. Later she feels differently and arises to open the door only to find him gone. Panicked, she goes and searches everywhere for him until they are finally reunited.

The story is applicable for today. Often our harsh responses teach others that it is better to look elsewhere for love and understanding. When we realize our foolishness and come running, the friendship may have vanished. Sometimes a diligent pursuit is necessary if the relationship is ever to bloom again. Words hold power. What we say can bless our friendships or destroy them.

A Word to Husbands

Much of nurturing the marriage relationship seems to fall on the wife's shoulders. Statistically far more wives seek marriage counseling than husbands, and they are often the first to sense that the marriage is in trouble. Is this as it should be?

We can point back to creation and appreciate the relational differences that are part of God's design. Sin marred that unity of the first man and woman and made role definitions necessary. Yet we can also point to the cross where Christ died proving the equality of men and women and tempering marriage roles with love. At Calvary, the husband's role changed. The Christian man is commanded to demonstrate sacrificial love for his wife. Christ's tender, unreserved love for the Church is his model (Ephesians 5:23-29). Practically, this means the quality of the marriage relationship rests foremost on the husband's shoulders—not the wife's. It means God expects him to lead the way in building the marriage relationship. Too often, the reverse is true.

Paul also speaks to Christian wives in this passage. He says: "Wives, submit to your husbands as to the Lord" (5:22). It sounds simple until you note the implied question behind the command: Husbands, how Christlike is your leadership in the home? The stark truth is this—that many wives would lovingly follow their husbands if the husband would take Christlike responsibility for the marriage.

Both Lover and Friend

Developing a rewarding marital friendship is hard work. Without God's enabling, none of us could pull it off. Without His perspective, we might easily bypass the friendship marriage offers. There are few things as rewarding as a marriage in which intimacy and passion have been woven together. God wants to make this your experience as well. After healing the rift between them, the couple in Song of Songs summed up the potential of marriage in a classic statement. They said simply, "This is my lover, this my friend" (Song of Songs 5:16). I hope you'll claim this as a goal for your marriage as well.

Endnotes

1. Doug Fields. *Creative Romance* (Eugene, OR: Harvest House Publishers, 1991), p. 15.

2. Melvyn Kinder and Connell Cowan. *Husbands and Wives* (New York, NY: Clarkson N. Potter, Inc., 1989), p. 172.

3. Ibid., p. 166.

4. Fields, p. 19.

Cheryl Smith is a pastor's wife, mother of two, speaker to women's groups and the author of two books, *From Broken Pieces to a Full Basket* and *Kindling a Kindred Spirit*. She has a B.A. in Christian Education from Biola University.

What Would They Do without Me?

taken from
Bounce Back, compiled by
Diana James

by Lola Gillebaard

If your kids are anything like mine, they believe their parents will always be around. They can't even stand for you to get sick. You're supposed to be there always, no matter what. Big babies, that's what they are!

Like many moms, I've always worried and feared for my kids. You know how it is: they may be six feet tall and approaching their thirties, as mine are, but they're still my "little" boys. If anything came along that threatened to hurt any of them in any way, I panicked. Like any good momma bear, my instinct was: "I've got to protect my cubs!"

Once in a while though, something happens that changes everything and gives you a whole new perspective. Like what happened when I found out I had breast cancer.

When I broke the news to my husband, Hank, my composure flew out the window, and I burst out crying. This was pretty hard on Hank, and I didn't want to do that again with my four sons. I fretted and wondered how I could tell them in a way that would not cause them trauma and distress. After due consideration, I decided to follow our usual family custom and just *blurt it out*!

Here's what happened when the first son called on the phone:

"Hi, Mom."

"Hi, babe."

"How are you?"

"Not too good. The doctor says I've got cancer."

Long silence.

"Gosh, does that mean you're going to die?"

Then the second son called.

"Hi, Mom."

"Hi, babe."

"What's up?"

"Nothing good, I'm afraid. I just found out I have breast cancer." Long silence.

"But Mom, why? You don't eat fat."

By the time the third son called, I was getting the routine down pat:

"Hi, Mom."

"Hi, babe."

"What's new?"

"Nothing good. I've just been told I have cancer." Long silence.

"I hope this doesn't upset Dad."

I could hardly wait to hear what the fourth son would say. Finally he called:

"Hi, Mom."

"Hi, babe."

"How's life treating you?"

"Not so hot. The doctor says I have breast cancer." Long silence.

"Darn. Why couldn't it have been Mrs. Walcott?" (Mrs. Walcott lived down the street from us and used to chase all the kids off her sidewalk yelling and brandishing her broom.)

Those deflating phone conversations took place on December 4, 1987, just before the Christmas season was getting into full swing. The next day, Saturday, I was to go in for a chest X ray and bone scan as a preliminary to a mastectomy scheduled for Monday. I told my family that if the doctors found the cancer had spread through my body, I would refuse the surgery.

Hank said he would stay with me during the X ray and bone scan. Now if anyone knows Hank, I know Hank. It worries me how he worries. I didn't want him out there in the waiting room pacing up and down, wearing holes in the hospital carpeting. I told him I could handle it just fine, thank you.

Saturday came, and I kept my lab appointment—without Hank. All day long, it seemed I did nothing but take off my clothes and put them on again. Off—on. Off—on. "So this is what it's like to be a model," I mumbled to myself.

I underwent each test inside a cubicle that would have made an igloo seem cozy and warm. The nurses glided in and out on their squeakless shoes, taking X rays or poking needles in my arms. Then they were gone, leaving me alone in my igloo, shivering with cold and terror.

My goose bumps were getting goose bumps when finally a group of long-faced men in white coats arrived to peer at me and prod me with their icy hands. After they left, I sat in numb fear, waiting for the doctor to come back and tell me the verdict. Had the cancer spread? The chances, I had been told, were 50-50 that it had.

Oddly, I began to realize that my fears were not about me. As usual, they were for my sons. I wondered what they would do if something happened to me. I thought of times they had disagreed and argued with each other and with their dad. I wondered how they would get along if I died and there was no longer a full-time peacemaker in the family.

I tried to pray. The prayer had trouble getting past the knot of terror in my throat. I began to picture my funeral. I saw our church with my family all sitting in the front row. There were flowers everywhere. Someone was reading the Twenty-third Psalm: "The LORD is my shepherd; I shall not want. . . ." The words that got to me were: "Yea, though I walk through the valley of the shadow of death, I will fear no evil: for thou art with me" (KJV). Those words stood out. They spoke to my soul. I repeated them quietly to myself, over and over. The room began to feel warmer, and the knot in my throat began to melt away.

Then suddenly the doctor was there. His voice, like the voice of an angel, flowed over me like a healing balm. "I see no sign of cancer in the rest of your body," he said.

I prayed that his vision was 20/20!

My spirits soared as I drove home. I wheeled into the driveway, jumped out of the car and ran toward our front door. The sound of music wafted from our living room.

24

Mahalia Jackson was there singing "Silent Night." (Well, it *sounded* like she was there.) I dashed inside. Standing in the corner of the living room was the largest Christmas tree we'd ever had. It was decorated with every ornament the kids had ever made—even the ugly ones.

Imagine, all this three weeks before Christmas, and I'd been away at the hospital lab for only five hours!

There, lined up in front of that huge tree, was my family. To my amazement, each one was wearing a suit and tie! I pushed back the thought that they looked ready to carry me down the aisle of the church—laid out in a box.

"Merry Christmas, Mom," they shouted in unison.

"Merry Christmas," I smiled, "and Happy New Year. We've got many more to come."

Hank and the boys and I all hugged each other as we sniffled and wiped away our tears. My four sons seemed suddenly taller, wiser and more mature.

In the midst of all this commotion, a great peace came over me. I wasn't fearful for my boys any more. A prayer silently formed inside me: *Thank You, dear God, thank You! I got Your message. You're always with me—and with my family. You've always been here, even when we "walked through the valley of the shadow of death."*

Then I noticed the dining room table was set with our best china, the good silver and all our precious chipped crystal.

I can tell it was one of the best evenings we've ever had together. God had never seemed so near. The family had never seemed so capable and caring. And take-out pizza never tasted so good!

Lola Gillebaard is a humorist, a college professor, author and professional speaker. Lola conducts training seminars on humor in the workplace and frequently serves as keynote speaker for corporate and convention audiences. She is a past president of the Greater Los Angeles Chapter of the National Speakers Association.

No Good Thing . . .

taken from
"Weak Thing" in Moni Land

by William Cutts

On our first furlough a reputable physician told us there was very little hope that Gracie would ever conceive a child, and if she did, only the most expert care would ensure the birth of a live, healthy baby. The officials at Alliance headquarters were sufficiently convinced of the accuracy of the prognosis that they eventually granted us permission to adopt up to two children to be on regular mission allowance.

It was true that many years earlier Gracie had been ruled out as ever being a biological mother, but as a result of the mumps, I now had slim chance of being a biological father. About May 1968, when Gracie was forty-four and I was fifty-three and we had been married for twenty-one years, the time arrived for the demonstration that nothing is too hard for our God.

Gracie began to be bothered with unusual symptoms of persistent nausea. She thought that she had some type of flu. The field conference was coming up, so she was looking forward to having a medical checkup at that time.

Gracie was examined by Dr. Thelma Becroft of the Australian Baptist Missionary Society as soon as an appointment could be arranged. She felt a lump in Gracie's abdomen and exclaimed, "What have we here? Have you felt life at any time, Gracie?"

"No."

"Well then, don't get too excited or breathe a word about it so that you won't be embarrassed. It could be a tumor. We must keep checking on it."

Gracie tried to be obedient, but she was pretty sure it was not a tumor. One evening, during a testimony meeting at the conference, Gracie stood up and made her famous birth announcement: "Bless the Lord, O my soul, and all that is within me, bless His holy name."

Dr. Becroft advised Gracie to have the baby in Irian Jaya, but I felt that we should consider the doctor's advice in 1952—that if ever she became pregnant, only the most expert care could bring a live, healthy baby into the world. It would be fine with me if William Albert Cutts, Jr., had my hair and two eyes the same color as my one, but I was determined to prevent his having a body like mine.

Dr. Becroft arranged for us to go to the hospital in beautiful Goroka, Papua, New Guinea, which is in the interior highlands about the same altitude as Hitadipa. At that time the most expert medical personnel in Australia took turns with a stint at the government hospital in Goroka. There was no way to ascertain when the baby would be born. Dr. Becroft said, "We'll just have to pull a date out of a hat." When we arrived in Goroka we thought we were about a month early.

The Summer Institute of Linguistics (SIL) people invited us to come to Ukarumpa, a town about fifteen minutes' flying time from Goroka for the waiting period. The SIL translators all have houses with modern conveniences at Ukarumpa. Each translator lives under very primitive conditions with the tribe whose language he or she is translating. After several months, having gathered reams of material, they return to Ukarumpa to process it. We thoroughly enjoyed our stay with them—the refreshing fellowship and the opportunity to discuss my translation problems with experts.

The gynecologist who examined Gracie upon our arrival at Goroka told us to be back there at a certain date for the birth. Dr. Ross had confirmed the prognosis of 1952: a natural birth could be very dangerous. "This little one is too precious to take a chance. I will do a Caesarian section."

It was a beautiful evening as I sat on the veranda waiting for our baby and praying. I didn't have too long to wait, for soon a small white blanket bearing William Albert, Jr., appeared. Elation, joy, thanksgiving, praise and worship filled my mind simultaneously as the tiny bundle was placed in my lap. "You have a little girl. Would you like to hold her until we get your wife cleaned up?"

It had never occurred to us that our baby might be a girl!

In order to get back into Irian Jaya, we had to send our passport to the American Consul in Jakarta together with a certificate of birth from Goroka and a photo. I brought my camera to photograph the new baby. Now we had to decide on a name for this little sweetheart. Eventually we agreed that the traits we sought—beauty, cadence, euphony, harmony—were implicit in the name Faith Elizabeth.

But that is not the end of the story. Thirteen months later we were back in Goroka going through the same routine. This time we returned to Irian Jaya with William Albert Cutts, Jr.

Many letters came addressed to "Abraham and Sarah Cutts, Hitadipa." A ten-year-old had a dormmate at the missionary kids' school at Sentani who observed, "When these missionaries find out that they can have babies, they keep having them and having them!"

> For the LORD God is a sun and shield;
>   the LORD bestows favor and honor;
> no good thing does he withhold
>   from those whose walk is blameless.
> (Psalm 84:11)

William Cutts, along with his wife, Grace, was one of the first missionaries to enter the interior of Irian Jaya (New Guinea). Their autobiography, *"Weak Thing" in Moni Land*, chronicles the tragedies and triumphs of their lives and ministry.

Baboo

taken from
Journey to Joy

by Marie Ens

The morning quiet was suddenly shattered by a huge blast. With Phnom Penh under siege we were getting somewhat accustomed to such sounds. Still, they always brought painful questions such as, "Who will have been hurt this time?" We certainly did not know in that moment that the answer to that question would change our lives forever.

A Khmer Rouge bomb had been secretly hidden in a pushcart full of fruit. The plan had been that the bomb would be propelled into the nearby army camp. But something had gone wrong. Instead of hitting the camp, the bomb merely shot across the road and exploded.

Mrs. Pay Yon had just been to visit her soldier husband stationed in the camp. She said good-bye and started off for home, her baby daughter in her arms. The child started to fuss, so Pay Yon sat down on a box in the street and nursed her.

Then it happened. The force of the blast flung the baby out of her arms and Pay Yon was hit in the head with a fragment of shrapnel. Someone had taken her to the hospital, convinced that she would not live.

We were informed that a mother, sitting in the street nursing her baby, had been killed.

If the nursing mother is dead the family will need baby formula, I thought to myself. I knew that World Vision stocked formula, so I set off to get some and try to find out where the family lived.

"I heard that the mother of a baby was killed," I said at the door of one house.

"No," came the answer. "She did not die. She was badly injured but she is still alive. She is in the hospital."

With my little gift of powdered milk I made my way to the hospital. What a sight met my eyes! There lay the mother, her head swathed in bandages, her arms tied to the bed rails. And by her side stood the father holding in his arms a sobbing little girl about ten months old. She wanted her mommy.

The father was beside himself, not knowing what to do. Suddenly I realized that this family needed a lot more than a few cans of powdered milk. Before I knew it I heard myself offering to take the baby home and care for her until the mother was well again.

And so it was that our house, emptied of children when our own all left for boarding school, again had a baby we could love. We called her "Baby." One day she tried to repeat her name but all that came out was "Baboo." So Baboo she became.

Baboo soon learned to walk. She also learned that if she reached up as high as she could at the piano she could make beautiful tinkling sounds. She looked darling in the little clothes I sewed for her. Our own children returned from school for Christmas break and were delighted with their pretend baby sister.

Finally Baboo's mother was released from the hospital and Baboo went back to live with her family. Pay Yon's injuries had indeed been severe, leaving her with one arm virtually useless and one foot that dragged along limply. She knew she could never keep up with a toddler and their little shack was near the river. We found out later that in order to assure her safety Baboo had been obliged to spend her days on top of the big wooden bed in the house. At least her mother knew where she was.

One day Baboo arrived back at our door. What a shock! Instead of the beautiful, cheerful child we had said good-bye to some months earlier, she was a sick, tragic-looking little girl.

We got medical help for her and found the family a more suitable place to live. We urged them to continue to bring Baboo to us if she ever got sick again and explained that it was essential to boil her drinking water to avoid recurring dysentery. The mother in turn explained to us that she was incapable of walking about to gather sticks to make a fire to do this.

One day the parents asked if we would consider adopting Baboo and raising her.

"She was really supposed to be yours," the mother said. "She got into the wrong reincarnation by mistake."

We loved Baboo very much but decided that instead of taking her away from her mother we would help raise her. We envisioned her growing into a beautiful teenager, having the advantages of a good education and perhaps learning to play the piano. And so it was that our house became Baboo's second home.

Once as I was typing a letter she crawled up and stood behind me on the chair. She was just tall enough to reach her arms around my neck from behind.

With her mouth next to my ear, she started to sing: "We ah one in da Spilit, we ah one in da Lah!" Yes! In English! How did she know that these strange sounds meant something to me, that the truth of what she was saying described the relationship that she and I enjoyed together? Yes, we did have a special relationship, our family and Baboo. Yes, we were one in the Spirit, one in the Lord.

Then came February 23, 1975. All the missionaries were given four days to prepare for evacuation. We kissed our little Baboo good-bye, our hearts refusing to believe that we would not be able to return to her and to Cambodia. No one dreamed that soon most of the little ones like Baboo would be dead, victims of Pol Pot's terrible massacre.

Safely back in Canada we often had a few leftovers after a family meal. *Just enough for Baboo*, I inevitably thought.

One evening we gathered in the living room to pray. Shelly prayed particularly for Baboo.

"Maybe," she exclaimed, "Baboo is already with You and she has the beautiful home that we always wanted her to have."

My heart was saying, "Precious little one, one day we will hug you again in that most beautiful of all homes!"

Marie Ens is a career missionary, having ministered in various countries in Southeast Asia and in France. After her husband's death in 1994, she returned to Cambodia where God has given her a ministry of hope and healing to the sick and the poor.

When a Father Abandons His Children

taken from the booklet
*When a Father
Abandons His Children*

by Ron Ballard

Recently in the city of Chicago an eleven-year-old African-American boy shot and killed a fourteen-year-old African-American girl in a park while trying to kill someone in another gang. Later he was found shot execution-style by fellow gang members. Prior to this he had had a long criminal record that communicated he was headed toward serious trouble.

One or two days later in a different city and community, a fourteen-year-old Anglo-American boy shot an eleven-year-old Anglo-American boy.

I cannot help but wonder—if the boys' fathers had been present in their lives, might these children be living today?

Many daughters turn to prostitution because their fathers abandoned them and left a void in their lives. So they begin to seek to fill this void by seeking love and attention from other men.

In this chapter you as a Christian father will be challenged to be the kind of father that God has called you to be, not to abandon your children but instead to leave behind a godly legacy.

When a Father Abandons His Children

In the African-American community nearly eighty percent of families are headed by single parents. Sixty percent of these are headed by women. Where are the men? For one reason or another, they have abandoned their children. This issue hits close to home for me because I was one of the above statistics, raised without a father.

The term "abandon" according to Webster's dictionary means to *forsake* or *desert*. You can forsake and desert your children both by moving out of the house *and* by living in the same house. Many live in the same house but do not function as a father; they are either too busy pursuing their own goals or they don't know how to function as a father. On the other hand, there are those who refuse to stay married to their children's mother and outright refuse to be a responsible father.

When children are abandoned by their fathers, it affects their ability to view God as their heavenly Father. Many adults have problems identifying with God as their heavenly Father because they cannot identify with their earthly fathers. Why do fathers abandon their children? Some of the reasons follow:

1. *Selfishness*—putting self first by being too busy doing their own thing, which may include playing the women, partying, pursuing a career and accumulat-

ing wealth. According to Isaiah 53:6, "All we like sheep have gone away; we have turned every one to his own way" (KJV).

When we please self, we cease to please God by not doing things His way. We are exhorted and commanded to put God and His righteousness first and other things will be given to us (see Matthew 6:33 and Deuteronomy 6:5).

2. *Insufficient employment*—many fathers do not earn enough to provide for their families, so they leave because welfare will provide sufficient funding to meet their family's needs. The welfare system can be both a blessing and a curse. Welfare helps provide shelter, food and clothing as a blessing. But if an employed man is in the house, welfare will not give assistance to a family. And separating families is a curse.

3. *Lazy and not responsible*—there are those men who are outright lazy and irresponsible. According to First Timothy 5:8, "But if any provide not for his own, and specially for those of his own house, he hath denied the faith, and is worse than an infidel" (KJV).

4. *Divorce*—some men, after divorce, begin living as if they do not have children. They develop "amnesia" where their children are concerned. One man, when told his children needed him, replied, "I have my own life to live and they will only complicate things." These men may refuse to call or visit—and so fail to take their place as father in their children's lives.

Biblical Mandate for the Father

God has given the father two primary responsibilities:

1. To teach children respect

Fathers should teach respect for the heavenly Father and authority as a whole. Ephesians 6:4 says, "Fathers, provoke not your children to wrath: but bring them up in the nurture and admonition of the Lord" (KJV). They are taught by seeing their father exhibiting a respect for the Lord in his life. According to Matthew 6:33, we are commanded to "seek ye first the kingdom of God, and his righteousness; and all these things shall be added unto you" (KJV). Let your children see that Christ is number one in your life and that you respect the government and other people, including your wife. As believers we are commanded to submit to one another and to obey our government. (See Ephesians 5:21 and Romans 13:1-4. May I add that this is true only as long as the government and others are not contrary to the will and Word of God.)

Children must also be taught to respect themselves. When children are taught that they are fearfully and wonderfully made, they will be able to respect themselves (see Psalm 139:14).

Children must be disciplined by their father. Proverbs 22:15 says, "Foolishness is bound in the heart of a child; but the rod of correction shall drive it far from him" (KJV). According to Proverbs 13:24, "He that spareth his rod hateth his son: but he that loveth him chasteneth him betimes" (KJV). "Chasten thy son while there is hope, and let not thy soul spare for his crying" (19:18, KJV). While disciplining, please do it in love and not out of anger. God commands us not to provoke our children to anger (see Ephesians 6:4).

2. To teach them how to be mature, responsible men and women

According to Psalm 78:5-8, God has commanded fathers to make known His Word to their children so that they might set their hope in God and keep His commandments. Fathers can teach children to be mature and responsible by

- encouraging children to study God's Word;
- helping them learn to pray;
- teaching them to make decisions by weighing pros and cons;
- encouraging them to spend time with the right kind of friends (Proverbs 1:8-19);
- expecting them to do their schoolwork.

Fathers should build godly character in their children. Character building is carving out the real person, the person your child is in the dark. We Christian fathers must do everything possible to teach and encourage our children to submit to Christ so that they might be transformed to His image (see Romans 8:29).

God's Order of Authority

Satan has attempted from the beginning to destroy God's order of authority by passing the man and going directly to the woman.

"And the serpent said unto the woman, Ye shall not surely die: For God doth know that in the day ye eat thereof, then your eyes shall be opened, and ye shall be as gods, knowing good and evil" (Genesis 3:4-5, KJV).

Instead of approaching the man, the God-designed authority in the home, Satan approached the woman.

It's the same way today—when salespeople want to make a sale, they will ask for the lady of the house!

When an earthly father abandons his children and their mother, he has ceased to be under the authority of the heavenly Father; as a result he leaves his wife and children vulnerable to the attacks of Satan.

The man is the covering and the protector of his family; when he removes himself from under God's covering or protection, the natural order that God has designed is disrupted. Many children are attacked by Satan and become thieves, drug addicts, alcoholics and even murderers. Satan comes to steal, kill and destroy according to John 10:10. And according to Mark 3:27, "No man can enter into a strong man's house, and spoil his goods, except he will first bind the strong man; and then he will spoil his house" (KJV).

Satan will capture your family and destroy them as long as he has you as the man in bondage, pursing your own ambitions and selfish desires.

Satan's Attacks

Learn from David

David abandoned his children by getting out from under God's authority. God commanded Israel not to take many wives according to Deuteronomy 17:17: "Neither shall he multiply wives to himself, that his heart turn not away" (KJV). But David disobeyed by taking on the following wives: Michal, the daughter of Saul; Abigail, the widow of Nabul; Ahinoam of Jezreel; and while living at Hebron he took four more wives! (see Second Samuel

3:2-5). Later, when he moved to Jerusalem, he took more wives and concubines.

David's sons saw their father's sexual sins and followed his example. David's son Amnon sexually abused his half-sister Tamar just as David took advantage of Bathsheba sexually. David's son Absalom, the full brother of Tamar, murdered his half-brother Amnon for raping his sister, just as his father David murdered Uriah, the husband of Bathsheba. Absalom went to Geshur, which was a heathen country, just as his father David went years before, disobeying the Lord by marrying the king of Geshur's daughter Maacah.

Because of David's sin, God said to him, "I will raise up evil against thee out of thine own house, and I will take thy wives before thine eyes, and give them unto thy neighbour, and he shall lie with thy wives in the sight of this sun" (2 Samuel 12:11, KJV). These words were fulfilled when Absalom had sex with David's concubines openly before Israel (see Second Samuel 16:22).

Absalom also tried to kill David and take over his kingdom. Lastly, two of David's sons died—Absalom was murdered and his first child with Bathsheba died.

What Kind of Legacy Will You Leave Behind?

If you knew that you were going to die within the next thirty minutes and you reflected back on your life as a parent, what would you say you've done to leave behind a godly legacy?

A legacy is something passed from one generation to the next. There are two types of legacies—an ungodly legacy and a godly legacy. According to Exodus 20:3-5, those who leave behind an ungodly legacy worship or serve other gods and pass their sins down to the third and fourth generations.

According to Deuteronomy 6:5-7, those who leave a godly legacy will love the Lord God with all their heart, soul and mind and will teach God's Word diligently to their children.

David's Legacy

Let us take a look at King David's legacy:

> Wherefore hast thou despised the commandment of the LORD, to do evil in his sight? thou hast killed Uriah the Hittite with the sword, and hast taken his wife to be thy wife, and hast slain him with the sword of the children of Ammon. Now therefore the sword shall never depart from thine house; because thou hast despised me, and hast taken the wife of Uriah the Hittite to be thy wife. Thus saith the LORD, Behold, I will raise up evil against thee out of thine own house, and I will take thy wives before thine eyes, and give them unto thy neighbour, and he shall lie with thy wives in the sight of this sun. For thou didst it secretly: but I will do this thing before all Israel, and before the sun. (2 Samuel 12:9-12, KJV)

David was told that calamity would be brought upon him out of his own house. Let us take a look at some specific sins in David's life to see how he passed his legacy on to two of his sons.

David's Sins

- committed adultery with Bathsheba;
- got Uriah drunk in the hope that he would go home, have sex with his wife and cover up David's sin;
- murdered Uriah by putting him on the front line to be killed;
- went to Geshur, a heathen country, and married Maacah, the mother of Absalom. He disobeyed God because God had said not to marry foreign women (see Deuteronomy 7:3).

His Children's Sins

- his son Amnon sexually assaulted his half-sister Tamar, David's daughter (see Second Samuel 13:14);
- his son Absalom got his half-brother Amnon, David's son, drunk so that he would not realize the danger that would come upon him until it was too late;
- Absalom murdered Amnon;
- Absalom went to Geshur, the same heathen country his father David went to;
- Absalom raised an army to dispose of his father, and David barely escaped;
- Absalom openly had sex with David's concubines.

By now it should be obvious that David left behind an ungodly legacy. Now let us take a look at Abraham, who left behind a godly legacy in his family.

Abraham's Legacy

God's promises to Abraham began with God calling him to leave his country and family to go to an unfamiliar place. Although he was from Ur, a pagan city that worshiped other gods, Abraham turned to the living and true God.

God's promises to Abraham were sevenfold, according to Genesis 12:1-3 (KJV):

1. I will make of thee a great nation;
2. I will bless thee;
3. I will make thy name great;
4. Thou shalt be a blessing;
5. I will bless them that bless thee;
6. I will curse him that curseth thee;
7. In thee shall all families of the earth be blessed.

Abraham's legacy affected eternity through his grandson Jacob whose name was changed to "Israel." Through Israel God infiltrated the earth in the flesh. The key to Abraham's legacy is that he believed God (see Hebrews 11:8-11 and Romans 4:20-21).

Although Abraham left a godly legacy, his life and family were not without fault. In the book of Genesis, it tells that as a result of a famine, Abraham went to Egypt with his wife Sarah and his nephew Lot. But while in Egypt Abraham and his family became corrupted. Abraham became a liar by saying his wife was his sister; his nephew Lot ended up in Sodom; and Abraham took Hagar as his mistress and had a son "out of wedlock."

Abraham's son Isaac was faced with a situation similar to the one his father had been in—should he lie about his wife or risk being killed? Isaac chose his father's way: "And the men of the place asked him of his wife; and he said, She is my sister" (Genesis 26:7, KJV).

What Kind of Legacy Will You Leave Behind?

Will you leave behind sophisticated pimps who live off women? Physical abusers who saw you abuse their mother and others physically and emotionally, with hitting, cursing and general disrespect? Will you leave a legacy of unfaithfulness? When you are unfaithful, you are saying to your children that it is OK to commit adultery. Have you abandoned your family? Family abandonment says to our children that it is OK for them to abandon their families.

Some Effects You May Have on Your Children

Your children will lack self-esteem and worth if they think that you didn't value them enough to hang around. They may be angry and bitter toward all people if they are bitter at you for leaving. They may have a problem trusting others for fear they will abandon them. Your daughters will have a problem trusting their husbands, fearing that they will leave. Your example tells your sons to abandon their families. Lastly, but most importantly, your children will have a problem seeing God as their heavenly Father because you were not around for them to see as an earthly father.

A psychologist by the name of Harold Voth, in his book *The Castrated Father*, says if the father is not the head of the family, there can be nothing but chaos. The father is responsible for structure, for form and for establishing the family standards, character, direction and strength. If he doesn't do these things, the family will be crippled.

The Solution to the Problem

Let us learn from David. Notice from Second Samuel 12:13 and Psalm 51 that David got back under God's authority by truly repenting of his sins.

Fathers, get back under God's authority by true repentance! This is done by agreeing with God that you blew it as a father when you abandoned your family. Change your heart and get aback under God's authority. Perhaps you cannot remove the scars in your family, but you can heal the wounds.

Tell your family you blew it as a father and ask for their forgiveness. Deep down in your children's hearts, they still long to be accepted by their father. I had a desire for my father to accept me as his child till the day he died.

How to Leave Behind a Godly Legacy

First, just as David did, we must confess and repent of our sins (see Second Samuel 12:13 and Psalm 51). Secondly, as Abraham did, we must believe God.

"Jesus saith unto him, I am the way, the truth, and the life: no man cometh uno the Father, but by me" (John 14:6, KJV). We must put our trust in Christ as our Lord and Savior and ask Him to break the power of an ungodly legacy. Hosea 2:6 says, "I will hedge up thy way with thorns, and make a wall." We should pray and ask God to stop an ungodly legacy by putting a hedge of protection around our families.

Lastly, we must patch up the holes in our lives by totally surrendering our lives to Christ. If there are leaks in our lives, the entire family will be affected.

God declared David "a man after his own heart" (1 Samuel 13:14, KJV). The Bible traces Jesus' physical descent back to David. God is ready to forgive you and raise up a godly legacy through you. "For thou, Lord, art good, and ready to forgive; and plenteous in mercy unto all them that call upon thee" (Psalm 86:5, KJV).

What kind of legacy will you leave behind? A *godly* or *ungodly* legacy?

Conclusion

God gave David his kingdom back and declared David a man after His own heart. God can restore your family, but like David, you need to repent! Before the great and dreadful day of God's judgment on mankind, He will send preachers who will "turn the heart of the fathers to the children, and the heart of the children to their fathers, lest I come and smite the earth with a curse" (Malachi 4:6, KJV). The message here is to repent of your sins.

Over 2,000 years ago Jesus Christ came and died on the cross in your place, taking upon His body your sins and the sins of the world. He was buried and rose again the third day. By putting your faith in the finished work of Christ, you can be restored.

You may place your faith in Him simply by acknowledging your failures, by changing your mind about sinning and by asking Jesus to come into your life as Lord and Savior.

Finally, a word of encouragement for those children whose fathers may never repent—the Lord will become your Covering and Protector. He will fill the void that is in your life. He promises to be a Father to the fatherless! (see Psalm 68:5). Several years ago the Lord filled the void in my life created by the abandonment by my father with these words: "When my father and mother forsake me, then the LORD will take me up" (Psalm 27:10, KJV).

General Douglas MacArthur once said, "I don't want my children to remember me as a general, but as a father who taught them to say, 'Our father which art in heaven, hallowed be thy name.'"

What do you want your children to remember?

Ron Ballard is the pastor and founder of Home Ministries Alliance Church in Dayton, Ohio. A graduate of Detroit Bible College, he holds a master's and doctoral degree from Bethany Theological Seminary.

Widow with a Husband

taken from
Please Leave Your Shoes at the Door

by Corrine Sahlberg

Dear Mom,

We are all fine ["all" included our four children—David, Evelyn, Dale and Esther]. Elmer came home after being away fourteen days. There was lots of work to catch up on—a door had fallen off the closet, an electric plug wouldn't work and we were out of most supplies—rice, flour, sugar and other cooking supplies.

Again, in April of 1963, I wrote to my mother:

Elmer will be home a total of eight days this entire month. I do a lot of reading! I wouldn't mind having a TV!

Again to Mom in 1964:

Elmer has been gone three weeks. Won't be home for three more weeks! Little Esther is good company. She keeps asking for Daddy. The children are OK—busy and happy at Dalat. It gets lonesome without Elmer here, but I keep busy making Thai teaching books, writing lectures and visiting our neighbors.

Married women missionaries of The Christian and Missionary Alliance are expected to be full-time missionaries. That policy brought me face-to-face with two important issues:

1. What was my responsibility to the children God had given us?
2. What was my responsibility to the work God had called me to?

I settled those questions shortly after we arrived in Thailand, when our first son, David, was just a baby. I chose to work in the city where we lived. In the city I could give the best care to our children and also do my best work for God. I knew I was doing what God wanted me to do.

Making that choice, however, meant I would be alone with the children for long periods of time. Elmer's evangelism work took him far out into the country areas. That kind of life—rough roads, danger of robbers and poor living conditions—I felt was just too difficult for the children. Finding suitable sleeping places and proper food for as many as six people, instead of one, would only complicate Elmer's ministry opportunities. Elmer could sleep almost anywhere and food was never a problem for him. So the "city missionary" and the "village missionary" learned to adapt. It was decided that when the last child went off to the mission boarding school, then I would travel with Elmer.

Coping with the "single-but-not-single" life was anything but easy. Just three months before the tragic death of the Johnsons, I took my first long train trip in Thailand without Elmer. I was traveling with two-year-old David while Elmer drove the Land Rover to our new home up on the border of Laos. The train left early in the morning and was scheduled to arrive in Udorn City at 6 that evening. Paul and Priscilla Johnson planned to meet me at the station. I would go to their home and Elmer would be there the next day.

Suddenly, however, the train stopped. I looked out the window. There was no station. All I could see were mountains and thick woods. Tall palms were silhouetted menacingly against the moonlit sky. *Why in the world would we be stopping in the middle of nowhere?* I wondered.

Soon a Thai conductor came through the car and stopped at our small compartment. David and I were the only foreigners on the train. The conductor said in English, "Train stop long time. You lock door. Close window. Keep light out. Stay here."

I pulled down the shutters on the windows and locked the door to our little room. Peeking through the shutters, I began to understand why the conductor had warned me about locking the door. Some of the male passengers were outside pulling bottles of liquor from their pockets. The conductor, evidently concerned about a young white woman traveling alone, wanted me out of sight of those men.

As the hours passed, more and more people left the train to sit outside. A train wheel needed major repair. It was going to be a very long wait.

I became a little nervous. I could hear a party in process in the moonlight. I prayed that the drunken men would stay outside. David and I ate our leftover lunch

51

sandwiches and drank from our water thermos. I was glad I had heeded the advice of an older missionary: "Always take water with you on trains, buses and in your own vehicle."

Around midnight the whistle blew and we were on our way again. The train pulled into Udorn at 2 a.m. Paul and Priscilla were waiting for us. They had made many trips to the station (there were no phones in those days). The stationmaster would only say, "Train will be late!" At midnight, they decided to remain at the station so they wouldn't miss me. Elmer arrived the next day and together we headed for our new home in Nongkai.

There was certainly plenty of city work to do in Nongkai. I started holding children's meetings, and when Elmer and the Thai preacher were away on village trips, I taught at the Sunday services and at the prayer meetings. It took hours and hours to prepare those lessons.

Another ministry began to develop for me. Students, nurses and even city officials requested English lessons. I told them, "I will teach you English, but I will use the Bible as the textbook." They agreed. Classes were held in our home and in government schools, still using the Bible as my textbook. I also spent hours selling Christian books and Bibles at our street chapel. The children and I talked to people, visited the food sellers along the sides of the roads and handed out tracts. Along the banks of the Mekong River, we watched the boats and chatted with the people who came to bathe there.

Looking forward to the time when Elmer and I would travel together in the villages, I prepared flannelgraph stories in large art books. But in spite of these ministries I

52

was often frustrated. A November 1954 letter to our field chairman, Mr. Chrisman, reveals some of my deepest feelings:

I received a telegram last night from Elmer. First news in seventeen days. The telegram stated, "Finished survey and meetings in Nongkai province. Now working in Loei province. Feeling fine. Love, Elmer."

Both of the children have had about the worst colds they have ever had, but we are all fine now. The Lord undertook in answer to prayer. I continue to teach at the services while a Thai girl watches the children at home. Greet Mrs. Chrisman for me. Tell her that when I start to feel a little lonesome (no white faces here in weeks), I think of how I planned to go to the mission field as a single missionary. Now at least I have Elmer some of the time. I also have two children to keep me company.

Mr. Chrisman replied,

Thank you for your letter. I am very proud of you and others who often have to do the hardest part of missionary work—sticking by the stuff while others go.

My journals reveal how I coped with "sticking by the stuff" for weeks at a time:

November 1952:

"Elmer plans a three-week boat trip soon with two missionary men. That will leave me the only American in this entire area. I'm not afraid to stay alone, though I'll miss Elmer. This is part of missionary life. Little David is good company—chats all the time."

August 1953:

"Elmer was off on a river trip when I became ill with terrible sharp pains in my side. He came home earlier than he had planned. I believe God sent him home to help me and take care of the children. We can hear bombing going on across the river on the Laos side. Many people have told us it is dangerous to be in Thailand, but I'd rather die out here in His will [than be anyplace else]."

When the papers were full of news about a possible invasion of Thailand, I became concerned because we lived near the border.

January 1954:

"I can still hear the bombs. Nongkai now has a special curfew. No one is allowed out after midnight or before 5 a.m. except with permission. No meetings of more than five people except with permission. Things are getting tense. Papers are full of the threat of an invasion. All kinds of measures are being taken to ward off such an occurrence. I am seriously considering moving down to Udorn but am waiting and praying to be sure this is God's will. If this area were to fall, I'd be the first missionary to know about an invasion! Soldiers would be at my door—no chance of escape. All the meetings have dropped in attendance; the chapel building might be sold. I might as well go to a place of safety. I think of the children. If I wait too long, it might be too late. I really hate to leave. Living at someone else's house will be inconvenient with the children, but maybe better than staying here. I wish I knew what to do."

I never did leave Nongkai.

February 1954:

"I can still hear the bombing in the distance but I sleep soundly at night. It is no fun staying alone so much, but God does give me a wonderful peace. My place is with the children. Sometimes I feel I accomplish so little, but just being faithful is an important thing."

April 1954:

"Elmer came home on Monday. He had planned to stay longer than nine days. I almost fell into his arms when he came in the door. I was at the end of my endurance.

"Evelyn has a terrible case of measles. As a result of walking the floor with her, my left arm pains me so much I can hardly hold her. The well caved in. I had to have water brought in on carts. The chapel building was sold. The Thai worker who lived upstairs in the chapel has no place to live."

It was too much for me. I went to bed and Elmer took over. The baby got worse, but Elmer was there to walk the floor with her.

November 1954:

"No lights and no Elmer! He has been gone almost a month. I am using kerosene lamps or candles until the city generator gets fixed. I am getting restless—a month is a long time to stay alone, but home is the best place for the children. Little Evelyn has been kissing Elmer's picture. The Lord is my peace and strength. I'm happy that Elmer is reaching those villages with the gospel."

Later that same month: "The lights were off three weeks. During this month I only saw foreigners three and half hours the entire month!"

Many, many times, over many years, I stood on the Mekong River bank and watched Elmer leave on a passenger/cargo riverboat. I never knew if he'd be gone a week or a month. When he returned, we would hear all about the trip: "I spent two and a half days on a twelve-by-twelve-foot bamboo raft. A trip through rapids on a raft is quite an experience! I don't know how the Thai men can judge the water so accurately, but they seem to know exactly when to start rowing to escape the huge boulders. I wished I could be as calm about it all as the cargo of pigs that accompanied us."

As furlough time drew near, I knew I needed a year in America. Four and a half years of life in Thailand had taken its toll. My journal records the frustration: "Another week and Elmer didn't come home. I am beginning to feel I can hardly stand another day alone. I'm discouraged with the poor attendance at the meetings. Although I keep busy, I am restless. I go for a walk every day. I feel I must walk. A lonely mission station is at times almost unbearable—so little to read, little (if any) mail (people seem to stop writing toward the end of a missionary's term) and no English programs on local radio stations. There is no one to talk with in my own language. Truly the Lord is a close Companion. If it weren't for the strength of the Lord and the everlasting arms, I could not stand the strain. The news reports are bad—trouble in Indochina and talk of war with China. The heat is terrific. Lately I always feel tired. I do need a furlough. I'm more nervous than I used to be."

A week later I wrote in the journal: "I spent a lonely Easter. After the Easter lesson, I spent two hours at the boat dock waiting for Elmer to come. The boat did not arrive. Elmer came home the next day—by bus. The boat for Nongkai was not able to leave, so he had to find another way to get home. I was so happy to see him. I just cried and cried. He did not realize how lonely I was. He says he'll take shorter trips now. There is much work to be done in the villages close by. It is so good to have someone to talk to."

There were times when I was concerned about Elmer's safety. The fighting across the river alarmed me enough that I wrote to our chairman, Mr. Chrisman. He had always told us, "Don't take unnecessary risks." And so I wrote:

I told Elmer I would be writing to you about what I feel is an "unnecessary" risk. A United States Army man advised us to stay around home now as anything could happen. He told us that if an emergency arose we would probably get on a U.S. Army plane in Udorn. I am not afraid to stay alone—I don't feel nervous—but I am wondering about Elmer going off on extended river trips during this time. I feel it would be safer for him to work here in the city or in villages close by. Please let me know what you think.

Mr. Chrisman answered,

It has been my intention to suggest that Elmer cease going on prolonged river trips. He should avoid overexposure to danger. While conditions are so uncertain, it seems wise to work in areas closer to home. I appreciate your eagerness to distribute the Word of God.

On January 1954, Elmer wrote the chairman:

River travel is closed now because of what seemed to be machine-gun fire on the river. I shall go only on day-long trips by Land Rover.

Later that year when the danger dissipated, Elmer was off again on river trips. In November 1954, obviously frustrated, I wrote my report to Mr. Chrisman:

Elmer has been gone about a month. His monthly reports and financial statements will be late. I refuse to do the station books because then he might stay out two months! Maybe, like Blondie in the Dagwood comics, I should have his suitcase ready with clean clothes as he dashes in and out of our house. Or maybe, since our Mission policy now is that single girls should not live alone, our conference ought to appoint another woman to live here!

I actually signed that letter "Miss" instead of "Mrs." because I lived alone so much of the time!

Although I was not usually bothered by fear, one incident remains fresh in my memory.

Elmer was out in the villages when trouble arose among the Vietnamese refugees in Nongkai. The government ordered the refugees to be fingerprinted, but they did not understand the reasoning behind the edict. Some of the men refused and were put in jail. So about

500 of their women gathered in front of the police station, squatting in typical fashion, to protest.

That night I could hear them screaming and crying all through the night (our home was only two blocks away from the police station). The next day, Saturday, the police used water hoses on the women in an effort to disburse them. I was the only American in the city and I knew that the Vietnamese did not like Americans. I sent a note with our Thai helper to the governor of the province. I told him that I was alone and asked him what I should do if things got worse. He advised me to stay inside the house and promised to send an escort to evacuate me if necessary. His assurance, as well as God's promise of protection, brought a measure of peace to my heart.

The loudspeakers were blaring an announcement: "All people who do not go home will be arrested." Then the message was directed to the local citizenry: "Thai citizens must stay off the streets. Be careful about drinking water from wells. There may be poison in the wells."

The next day, Sunday, I looked out of my window just as a group of wailing women were marched past our house. Six armed Thai policemen were forcing them to go back to their homes.

The government gradually got things back to normal and peace returned to the area. I was thankful for the people who prayed for us.

There were different ways of coping with the problems the children and I faced. I was happy for my medical training which helped when the children were sick. Also, I kept busy, not allowing myself to sit around and think about things I could not change.

Reaching out to other people kept me from feeling sorry for myself and I had the habit of walking every day. This discipline was good for both the body and mind. Photography, writing and reading helped me relax. Besides all that, I never really felt alone. God was very real to me during those years.

I remember how surprised a woman in the States was when I responded to her question concerning how I faced problems on the mission field.

"Who did you go to when you had a real problem?" she asked.

"I went to God!"

"No, no," she replied. "I mean a person."

I explained, "Where I lived there was no one but God. For years, even my husband wasn't around much of the time. God was a very real Person to me. He met my needs."

As I checked through the thirty-five years' worth of letters I had written to my mother, I was surprised at the length and frequency of Elmer's village trips. No wonder the Thai people called me *Maamy tee me saame*—the widow with a husband!

Corrine Sahlberg, missionary, wife and mother, spent thirty-five years in Thailand. Her autobiography, *Please Leave Your Shoes at the Door*, chronicles the faithfulness of God in the life of a family whose dogged determination enabled them to serve Him no matter what the consequences might be.

Under the Same Roof

Teaching a Skill

taken from
To Be a Father Like the Father

by Michael Phillips

"**M**ama, Mama—I can do it!" Our little boy came steamrolling onto the small deck where we were having a refreshment break. In his delicate hands he carefully cradled an almost-full can of soda, making my wife and me instinctively want to grab the can away from him before any of it spilled on his grandparents' new veranda. But we could see by his steeled expression that he had a death grip on the can.

"What can you do, John?" I asked. He raised himself up to full height and stuck out his chest with pride.

"I can drink with a straw!" he announced. "Uncle Glen showed me how." Then as if we were still neophyte unbelievers, he guzzled and slurped up as much liquid as his mouth could hold. We watched his cheeks expand until they looked like they would explode. Then when he had sucked all he could hold, he downed it in one gulp.

If you've ever swallowed a carbonated drink that way, you'll know what comes next. He looked shyly up at his mother, and with a grin touching the corners of his mouth, he said softly, "Uncle Glen showed me some-thing else, too." Then he paused in a way not unlike a boxer ready to unload a stiff right hook and let go a gigantic burp! Kathy and I both reacted at once, though with vastly different comments.

I said, "John, that's disgusting."

"Where's Glen?" Kathy asked, "I'm going to kill him."

And off she went to commit unclecide. When she was gone, I told my son not to burp like that again in front of his mother.

If I had known then what I know now about the male members of my extended family, I never would have let any of them close to my boys!

My brother taught my youngest son how to spit and how to make it hang together for better distance. My father-in-law passed on the time-honored and hallowed family tradition of making rude and annoying armpit noises. Kathy's brother showed my sons how to make even more delightful sounds using their lips and their arms.

They have also showed them more innocuous skills such as drinking directly out of a carton of milk, eating cold pizza for breakfast and screaming at the top of their lungs when their favorite football team scores a touchdown. None of the family members have ever charged anything for passing on these skills.

Nor would I pay them if they had!

The passing on of skills from parent to child is not as simple as the above pseudo-examples. Great thought and effort must go into every attempt at skill teaching and acquisition. The most meaningful skills that human beings must learn are also the hardest to pass on. Loving, nurturing, achieving, sustaining, rebuilding, dreaming and working are all processes that, by their nature, require hundreds of attendant skills. We may even give up, as some parents have, and assume that certain skills are attained by experience rather than by modeled behavior.

"He Never Taught Me Nothing"

Gaston grew up knowing two things about his father: First, he worked hard to support his wife and kids (he told them this daily); and second, the first thing was all he knew about his father. He told me that when he was in trouble at school, he would go to his dad for advice. But his father only got angry at him and told Gaston to leave him alone.

For years Gaston was segregated from his father. His mother tried desperately to bring her husband and children together, but he never would have much to do with them. The man was a closed book. Gaston related one incident that later became monumental to his well-being. He asked his father where babies came from and how they were made.

His father's answer was a slap in the face: he was told that he wasn't supposed to think about those things. As he entered puberty, his urges were as powerful as his mind was ignorant. As a result of this, he allowed himself to become involved with a group of boys who would regularly abuse him homosexually. When he tried to speak to his dad about the matter, he was shoved away.

Years later, when I was helping him pick up the pieces, he would often cry profusely. In his tears, he would mutter a salty wish that his father had done something to help him grow up. His most bitter moment came prior to his complete healing. He looked at me with eyes that were distended and red from crying. With a look of utter hatred he said, "He never taught me nothing—not one bloody thing!"

What a sad and tragic story. In the field of responsibility training, a parent is grooming a child to learn the value of the proper responses in life. The ultimate goal is to bring a child from irresponsibility to the point where he will act with intelligence and wisdom. Skill training does not look at an *irresponsible* child; it sees an *untrained* child. Its goal is to set down standard operating procedures that will adequately aid the child in living life successfully.

In Gaston's case, the father passed nothing down to his son, not even the barest scraps needed for survival. Since the family structure prevented Mom from being helpful, Gaston was on his own in a hostile world.

Daniel Asa Rose, in a brilliant essay on the meaning of fatherhood called "Spring Training," says this:

> For two and a half decades, my father stood in as mankind to me. Whether he knew it or not, I invested mad amounts of energy both battling and celebrating this figure who seemed single-handedly responsible for making the world as imperfect as it was, and occasionally as fine.

In Rose's description of life with his father, he pictures a scene where the rest of the world falls back as a relief background and real life exists in the battles and blessings of how his dad tried to direct his life. Now Rose is the father, and he wonders about his own son:

Now it's I who personifies history to my own son. This whippersnapper who steals second base watches me with hawklike brilliance, obsessing over my shortcomings, marveling at my occasional displays of wit. Now when I press Marshall's reluctant fingers on the piano keys, it's not because I think the baroque is great but because how else will it be passed down. Now when I put my teenage trophies in his room, I do it not to dwarf him but—so obvious!—to give him someone to look up to.

Indeed, how does anything get passed down unless the fingers of the father are pasted upon those of his child? There is no replacement for the moment-by-moment mentoring that a father can give to his children. Even when he is tired, there are skills to be taught about the proper ways to handle and view rest and recreation. To a child, the whole world is distilled into the details and grand motions of his dad's life.

Jesus puts this truth succinctly when He describes His relationship with the heavenly Father in John 5:19: "I tell you the truth, the Son can do nothing by himself; he can do only what he sees his Father doing, because whatever the Father does the Son also does." The universe revolves around Father-God, and the Son of God is acknowledging that there is no one better to observe than the skilled Father at work.

Father-God is the perfect model in the realm of skill acquisition. John 5:20 goes on to say, "For the Father loves the Son and shows him all he does. Yes, to your amazement, he will show him even greater things than these."

There we have it. This is the template of true skill teaching. Father-God loves His Son. He takes the skills He possesses and, in an ever-increasing way, displays them carefully so the Son can copy them. As followers of God, our human fathering must begin with the assumption that true love seeks to prove itself in the teaching of skills in every facet of life.

While gathering material for this book, I happened to have dinner with my brother who, at the time, was doing a family history for a course he was taking to get his master's degree in family counseling. Without knowing it, his questions caused me to think of an experience with our father. At first glance, I thought Dad had been unnervingly negligent in this arena of skill training. But as we reminisced, we both came to a fresh appreciation of the volume of life he had passed down to us. Quite apart from mere genetic throw-overs, we have gained much from our father. And the more I think about it, the longer the list of skills that can be traced to him becomes.

Some of these I've included in the next few pages; most I have not. More important, what's delineated here is a bare outline of where God has brought His children through the ages and where human fathers can and should journey with their children.

Bathroom Skills

Skill training starts early, almost from the moment a child is born. Does that sound ludicrous?

Lydia Dotto, in her book *Losing Sleep*, cites several scientific studies done on the sleep patterns of newborns. The conclusions of the studies confirm that a parent can begin training a child to sleep through the night from the first night after its birth. Though a baby does not develop a sense of circadian (a twenty-four-hour period) cycles until he is three or four months old, he is still able to comprehend what is expected of him during waking and sleeping patterns.

My wife, a licensed practical nurse, has a theory about nocturnal sleeping that has proven successful with our kids. After working in pediatric and obstetric wards, she observed that most babies are bathed during the night shift rather than during the more hectic moments of the day. Therefore, these tykes were being deceived into thinking that the night part of the cycle was for being awake.

So, with our own, Kathy requested that the nurses not wake up the babies at night; she would bathe them during the day. After coming home, my wife and mother-in-law took turns getting up with each child as they aroused during the night. Instead of milk, they fed them water (which they also need, by the way). Our first son slept through the night after one week. The second and third children were not as compliant, but after a month they both snoozed at the prescribed time.

Please note: This is not the Phillips Proven Theory for Newborn Care. See your own doctor and do your own thing. The point is that even a newborn can be trained to follow the basic skills of life.

I call these elementary habits "bathroom skills," because a good majority of life's essential lessons revolve around the toiletries. Brushing of teeth, combing the hair, washing faces and lifting the toilet seat are essentials that no parent would think of leaving untaught. Other issues might include dressing oneself, what to eat, when and how much to sleep, how to talk on the telephone, how to walk and how not to leave gum on the chair when Daddy is sitting down to write (a very recent lesson).

God is not above teaching these kinds of things. In Genesis 3:21 He does His first fatherly deed for His children after sin has entered their lives: "The LORD God made garments of skin for Adam and his wife and clothed them."

Though this is not a favorite memory verse, the message is significant, especially when we consider that it was the first thing God taught man after the Fall.

God could have sat Adam down and begun training him in theology, reading, sociology (there was coming a "socio" to "ologize" about) and any number of useful curricula. But instead, He sat His son down and showed him the fine art of tailoring. We have to assume that God did more than just make Adam a set of clothes. Adam had to learn quickly that if he were to survive in a world where heat and cold and even shame abounded, clothes were necessary. God also relayed another principle to His son: *basic living was going to be hard.*

Matthew 6:31–32 has this to say about our basic needs:

> So do not worry, saying, "What shall we eat?" or "What shall we drink?" or "What shall we wear?"

For the pagans run after all these things, and
your heavenly Father knows that you need them.

While this is a popular portion of Scripture, it can be
misleading. Apart from manna and a few group feeding
parties that Jesus hosted, it seems that God doesn't *just
give* us the essential things in life; we must expend effort
to get them. I think this indicates that our heavenly Father will do all He can to ensure that we are trained
properly in the acquiring of the essential skills in life.

That is why God created the family. In essence, it would
forever be Adam's responsibility, and every father's who
came after him, to systematically impart the initial living
skills to his children. God showed Adam the most necessary skills: making clothes and obtaining food from the
carcasses.

Drill Sergeants

Are the "bathroom skills" worth talking about? It
seems so incredibly obvious that a child has to learn to
eat, sleep, walk, talk and hang up his coat on a hanger.
Yet there are good parents everywhere who assume
these skills should just arrive by something akin to a
spiritual courier service. We say things like "Where is
your head at?" and "How can you do that?" These rhetorical questions suggest a child should know something that we have never adequately taught him.

For most children nothing comes naturally. They are
given to us as bundles of utter chaos and inexperience.
Acting as proverbial drill sergeants, we must whip them
into shape. The war we're getting them ready for is life.

71

My stepfather and mother have worked in a group home for the mentally handicapped. I also have had several close friends who worked in institutions that cared for the mentally disabled. When they have described their duties to me, I thought their work must often be unpleasant—and futile. Teaching a thirty-year-old how to tie his shoes, or an eighteen-year-old how to go to the bathroom, seems to me to be the height of hopelessness. Yet Mom and Dad's example of working in a group home has communicated something to me of extreme importance. If you take the time, effort and loving care to keep teaching a "bathroom skill" until it is learned consistently, even the disabled person can function in our world.

But the reverse is true as well. Even the brightest child, if given inferior training in the essentials of life, can be severely disabled in dealing with normal living conditions.

This is hard to admit, but one thing I never was much concerned about was body odor. My own odor never bothered me, and I guess my mother felt it was not her place to say anything to me about it. Oh, she would occasionally wave her hand in front of her face when I was near her, but I concluded, as did many of my friends, "That's just Mom." I loved Dad dearly and know he did his best to be part of our lives, but when it came to the essentials in life, he never said much. As a result, during puberty's sweat-producing years, I had many embarrassing moments that I didn't know enough to even be embarrassed about.

One day after French class my ravishing teacher took me aside. I thought she was going to praise my good

grades. Rather, she told me that I wasn't cutt.
grade—socially—and that several of my friends h.
asked her to speak to me about my underarm odor.

She mentioned deodorant. My mother had bought
me a can and regularly encouraged me to use it. But I
didn't think it was necessary.

"Miss Gorgeous," the French teacher, burst my balloon.
That day I went to the store and invested in a new can of
scented deodorant. Only once, when I was too broke in
college to even afford deodorant, have my precious pits
gone without. Who knows, I may never have gotten close
to being married if it were not for my French teacher!

Father-God didn't mind getting down to the basics.
He probably explained to Adam why this kind of clothing was necessary. Human fathers should take a hint
and on a sheet of paper list the elementary skills that go
into living in this world. Then they should check off how
many their children have mastered. The rest of the list is
your challenge as a father to teach to your children.

Brotherly Love Skills

The prophet of God sat down wearily on the rock.
The toil of watching his people decimated by war and
ruin was hard enough for any Israelite to bear. But because he was God's man, others turned to him for an answer in the midst of annihilation. However, there was
one problem with their expectations. God wasn't saying
anything! While mothers clutched dead infants to their
bodies and sons cried to heaven for their fathers who
lay in fractured heaps at their feet, Jonah only received
silence as an answer to his desperate petitions. He

could not comprehend how God could allow His people to be treated with such ferocity by the Assyrian invaders. It was a dejected man who dawdled by the road that day, perhaps feeling as if his Father in heaven had rejected him most of all.

"Jonah," an inner voice called. "Jonah, I must speak to you, son. Will you listen?" The inner compulsion he had always comprehended as God's voice now shouted urgently within his mind. *Here is the answer we've been waiting for*, he reasoned as he prepared to hear God.

"Go to the great city of Nineveh and preach against it, because its wickedness has come up before me" (Jonah 1:2). After that came the knowledge of His anointing resting upon Jonah, God's spokesman.

But unlike other missions the Master had sent him out on, this one did not fit well. He had no problem with the destination—Nineveh was ripe for God's judgment. They deserved a Sodom-and-Gomorrah-like cataclysm for the insane destruction they had inflicted. Jonah also didn't have much of a problem with the message itself. Not really. He knew that they needed to hear of the approaching doom about to explode in their midst.

It was the "forty days" he couldn't accept. He was not a sophomoric prophet who was unaware of God's purposes. If God was sending him to preach a punishment yet forty days away, then He had one prime objective in mind: He wanted them to repent! The thought of God offering forgiveness to those barbarians sickened Jonah. His rising indignation bloomed into both fear and abhorrence, fear because God might not allow him any choice in this mat-

ter and abhorrence for God's plan that thwarte
thoughts of revenge.

So he made a decision—God wanted him to go e
he would go west. He quickly booked passage on a boat
going as far west as the world went—to Tarshish, which
literally means the end of the world. He wanted to be
anywhere but in the midst of this plan God had devised.

Most of us could prosaically finish Jonah's journey. The
sea comes to get Jonah through storms, sailors and a giant fish. After the fish spat him ashore like a beached bar-
nacle, he was disciplined, chagrined and much the worse
for having traveled the maritime route. Actually, though it
came as small consolation to Jonah, his fish-belly experience would greatly help his mission to Nineveh.

What can we conclude from God's inventive way of
veering Jonah back on His course? Obviously, no one can
escape God's demands on his life. But does God really
need to go to such exorbitant lengths to prove a point?
The real reason God brought Jonah to Nineveh through
such circumstances comes out in the final chapter.

In chapter 4, Jonah complains to God, "I knew that
you are a gracious and compassionate God, slow to anger and abounding in love, a God who relents from
sending calamity" (4:2). God needn't have wasted the
mercy lesson on Jonah. He already knew all about it.
That's why he took off. Jonah continued in his pity party
and headed out of town to mope.

It's a typical childlike behavior and one that can result in serious consequences as it grows into bitterness. Father-God could not allow His son to give in to

75

such resentment, so He enlists some *helpers* to teach the prophet a lesson.

He used the sun to "bake" Jonah until he was roasted. In Jonah's bleached-out condition, the heat would have been painful.

The Lord then used a vine to provide shade for our hero. And finally, a worm came and ate the vine, leaving Jonah where he started—hot!

Jonah feels God's presence and complains. God asks him if he feels his complaint is worth pursuing, and Jonah replies in the affirmative. Now for the punch line.

God said to Jonah, "You have been concerned about this vine, though you did not tend it or make it grow. . . . But Nineveh has more than a hundred and twenty thousand people who cannot tell their right hand from the left. . . . Should I not be concerned about that great city?" (4:10–11).

Because Jonah wrote the book, we can assume that he got the point, which is this: God wants to show loving-kindness and mercy and desires to teach His children (prophets included) that brotherly love is God's way.

As a father, I don the referee's cap more often than I care to. Why? To quell conflicts between our children. And believe me, I know from experience that sibling rivalry equals any multinational confrontation anywhere. In our house it always leaves my wife and me saying, "Why can't they get along?"

How does God model brotherly love skills? In short, He forces His children into relationship challenges. Examples of this abound throughout the Scriptures:

- Joseph and his brothers

- Isaac, Jacob, Esau and the blessing
- David and King Saul
- Ananias and Saul (Paul)
- The Greek widows and the apostles (see Acts 6)
- John Mark and Paul

In each of these cases, God orchestrated the events with precision so that the protagonists are faced with the choice of behaving either in a loving manner or selfishly. In most of these cases there was a penchant for selfishness. But even when there was a retreat from brotherly love, God didn't give up on the training process. He waited a bit, then put His children together again in order to see if they had learned the skills of loving others. No matter how many times Saul breathed out threats against David, God kept bringing them back together. Despite the unthinkable cruelty Joseph's brothers did to him, God brought them together finally. Though Paul was disappointed with John Mark, God united them. (We even read in Second Timothy 4:11 that Paul said that John Mark became a useful and trusted companion.)

Treating Mother Properly

Recently, I took a week of vacation just so I could spend time with my family. We did jigsaw puzzles, read books, discussed science projects, played family games and did anything else the kids wanted to do (outside of watching television). We had a "togetherness" week.

By the second day we were all ready to do each other in. Competition in the games reached a feverous pitch. Our youngest child wanted to do something different every five minutes—just as the rest of the family was gaining an interest in a particular activity. Kathy and I wanted to do more adult things; the kids wanted to do more kid things. We were a mess, and I knew it.

I left the house intending to get some fresh air and tranquility. What I received was some advice from my heavenly Father. He pointed out to me that the main problem was that we were five people vying for each other's visual and auditory attention. No one was playing the role of referee or captain. It was a free-for-all family recreation explosion that was wounding the participants.

Arriving back home, I quietly began working to change things. I took time to establish some family-time rules, then Kathy and I split up the team, with one of us reading and the other playing soccer.

But one of my sons continued to act contrary, especially toward his mother. I took him out for a drive and stopped at a park. I coaxed him into telling me some of the hang-ups he was having. He poured out his heart, and I listened. Then I pointed out some of his boyhood peccadilloes, and he agreed he needed to treat his mother with more respect. I had an idea, so I tried it out on him.

"Why don't you watch how I treat Mom, and you treat her the same way?" His visage brightened, and he expressed eagerness to try out this modeling exercise. After the week was over, Kathy commented to me that the two of them were getting along much better.

Every human being needs to be taught how to act in an unselfish manner. Selfishness is the core of sin's grasp over our being. Father-God's example points out the need to examine the social development of our chil-

dren and to determine where selfishness n[...]
curbed.

The ways parents do that are many, but God's favorite way is to put us in various relational arenas, and then give us the ways and means to work things out ourselves.

Employable Skills

Leo Buscaglia, a best-selling author and public speaker, tells about the impact his father had in helping him choose a profession. Every night, his father would finish dinner and then stare at his children. They knew the question he was about to utter, for he had asked it every night. A favorite query was "What did you learn today?" The children could not plead ignorance; it was no excuse in the Buscaglia house. Those who occasionally tried this approach would be answered, "There is so much to learn. Though we're born stupid, only the stupid remain that way."

No fact was too trivial for the dinner table. If all they learned was the name of the capital city of Nepal, it was more than enough. Papa was satisfied.

When Leo migrated from home to the halls of higher learning, he saw how great a gift his father had supplied him with:

> When I finally emerged from Academia, generously endowed with theory and jargon and technique, I discovered to my great amazement, that my professors were imparting what Papa had known all along—the value of continual learning. (*Reader's Digest*, September 1989)

My father said it differently: "If you find someone who knows more than you do—and you will—pick his brains until you find out all that he knows." He would announce this to me often, for I had a major character flaw while growing up: I thought I knew everything.

Dad would often come home and read several newspapers from cover to cover. My most delightful memories of this presupper ritual were that he would often throw out tidbits to me. Long before trivia was in vogue, my father grasped the significance of the seemingly benign events that took shape around us. The stories he pulled out smacked of pathos, triumph and the human condition.

He often asked me what I thought of the story. He quietly listened to my opinion and then, without contradicting me, would sally forth with his version of the events. They were indeed eventful. He added color to the drab and pedestrian stories of average people doing archaic things. What I learned from these newspaper seminars was to be fascinated with people. It was probably by his side that I decided to become a doctor. People's diseases were an extension of themselves, and they needed excision—and study!

However, I never became a doctor. But not one bit of Dad's pedagogy was wasted. When God's call came upon my life to be a pastor, what stoked the burning fire was my desire to study people and their quirks. The Bible became a feast of foibles and follies, a tribute to the worst that man could be. My father's lifetime study of humanity was passed down to me in a way he nor I ever dreamed.

Without intending it, he gave me an employable skill. He imparted an instinct that all the institutions could

match. Part of the reason Dad's tutelage was so ef-
in that he went where no school can possibly go:
articles a̲ ̲n̲i̲n̲g̲ of my life.
thers raised c̲ ̲ ̲ this book, I read dozens and dozens of
of learning the lo̲v̲ ̲ phies relating to the way certain fa-
Writers such as Buscag̲ ̲mous) children. Carpenters spoke
from their fathers. I read a̲ ̲ilding at their father's knee.
challenged to create, painters wh̲o̲ ̲ed the quest for learning
ing what no one else was seeing, ̲ ̲performers who were
learned a decided love for people by looki̲ ̲re coerced into see-
triarchs. ̲ ̲ng at their pa-

I am not just speaking of direct, transferable crafts
when I refer to "employable skills." Almost anything
that a father gives a child by way of a definable art or
method can be used as a skill. My dad had no idea that
his newspaper tidbits would build into me a habitual
way of seeing people. But whether he intended it or
not, what he gave me is used in my preaching, counseling, writing and even managing the church office.

God set an example for this in the life of Moses. Most
of us know the story well. The first stage of his life was
as auspicious as it was dangerous. He was born in the
middle of a deadly decree: all Hebrew boys were to be
destroyed by the edict of Pharaoh. The king was afraid
that the prolific Jews would out-populate the Egyptians.
Moses' mother, not wanting to see her son murdered,
sent him sailing down the canal in a reed boat. Sister
Miriam was sent to watch what happened to the child.
The story took an interesting turn at this point. One of

Pharaoh's daughters, who happened to ..ld the picked up the basket and found the baby.. It was love—maternal love—at fir.. point on, woman decided to adopt the boy, ..d famous." We Moses' lifestyle was that of "the ..ership skills in this can assume that he learned g..d his real mother, who household. All the while, ..e also can assume that she earlier had cared for hi.. ..eritage, stories about Abraham, told him stories of b.. these two households, God com- Isaac and Jacob. .. the circumcised with the law of order bined the love .. and might this became a potent combination.

However, before he was mature enough to be both leader and teacher of Israel, Moses tried out for the position anyway. He killed an Egyptian who was beating a Hebrew slave. Word got out to the authorities, and Moses fled the scene. So far his "employable skills" weren't much use.

Moses spent the next forty years in the sheep business. The Bible doesn't tell us much about those years. But how much can you say? His diary would have been pretty scant.

In this tedium he put down his rash boldness and developed a calm, day-by-day attitude. When God came to put him into his real life's work, he was as humble as a person can be. Actually, he was too humble. It took miracles, promises and even an assistant prophet by his side to coax Moses on.

But Moses went, finally. And in the next forty years or so, he was required to use all of his learned skills: the boldness of a ruler, the wisdom of a trained Hebrew, the patience and tenacity of a shepherd. Because he also had learned humility, he gave the glory to God.

God gave Moses every skill he needed to have an advantage in life. Human fathers can share the best of their abilities, hoping that some of them will be sufficient to use in making a living.

Transferring Life-Skills

I believe the secret is to take time to show our children all we know about the life-skills we are good at. For instance, my father taught me everything he knew about golf. He had spent many years perfecting his knowledge, and what he learned he passed on to my brother and me. He would teach us stances, grips, putting and hitting out of sand traps. He passed on etiquette, respect, grace in losing (sometimes) and the challenge to improve. It was one thing he did very well in life.

When he died, I stopped playing golf for ten years. My brother, Dave, never did stop, and now he is an excellent golfer. But when I started playing again, the game had a different flavor to it. I was an adult, and I had to do more with this sport than just waste time at it. God has shown me two ways to use golf that have enhanced my ministry.

First, it is a surefire way to relax when things at the church are getting to me. I believe I've been able to live on an even keel because of God's ministry to me through golf.

Second, the game is a perfect setting for Christian fellowship. In the last year alone, I have established many contacts and struck up many conversations (with Christians and non-Christians alike) that have added to the effectiveness of our church's ministry.

Some of you may be thinking you don't have many skills—at least any that are of importance. But all of us learn hundreds of skills in the process of living life. If we pass each of these on to our children, then they will have an arsenal of techniques and knowledge that may combine together in some unique ways.

In the last two years, I have taught my kids gardening, football, guitar, singing, hiking, map-reading, writing and computer skills, how to change the oil in the car, how to cook omelettes, how to prune the apple tree, how to mow the yard, cement mixing, hammering a nail, how to use a photocopier, how to write a thank-you card, newspaper reading (a family tradition), how to exercise, how to kick a soccer ball, golf, Bible reading, tithing and how to take care of fish. My wife has taught them hundreds of other skills, too. I found that teaching these skills was relatively simple if I developed a plan. Here's what I found out:

1. Know what you want to teach.
2. Show them what to do.
3. Let them try it.
4. Show them how to do it better.
5. Let them try it again.
6. Keep showing them more intricate details.
7. Let them try it again.

I believe that God showed Moses so many examples of leadership styles because He wanted him to be the consummate leader. God modeled anger, compassion, loving care, rebukes and judgment. Then He let Moses try it himself.

Dating Skills

For this delicate subject, we need to travel again to the Garden of Eden. In Genesis 2:18, we read about God's concern for His son Adam: "The LORD God said, 'It is not good for the man to be alone. I will make a helper suitable for him.'" God had made Adam so that he would freely and uncoercedly seek God his Father. It remains a mystery why God wanted man's company. But He did desire Adam's friendship, and He did His utmost to maintain strong ties. Did it make sense, then, to break up this solid, one-on-one relationship by creating a woman so shapely and desirable that she would draw Adam's head away from his Father?

In my amazement, I realize that God made the eventual sexual and spiritual union of His son Adam with Eve a *goal!* He invented them in such a way that they would want to be together.

Genesis 2:18 describes Eve as a "helper." The word "helper" is an unusual Hebrew word. Many translators have put forth the inherent ideas of partner, helper, assistant and aide-de-camp. But it's a word that suggests someone who comes rushing to your side in times of trouble.

If I were God, I would have sequestered Adam from anyone else he wanted to relate to. I would have prevented there being anyone else to relate to. But, thankfully, I'm not God. The main thought here, though, is that God is not threatened by Adam's attraction to Eve; He wasn't worried about the dating that would ensue.

Adam's first word when he saw Eve, translated into English, was "Wow!" Now God wasn't the only attraction in Adam's life. What causes me to take another admiring glance at my heavenly Father is that He wasn't threatened by Eve. God could have invented Nintendo instead, and Adam wouldn't have been one bit wiser.

Let's take a hint from Father-God: Part of our job as fathers is to infuse our children with the excitement, knowledge and skills they will need to relate to the opposite sex. If at all possible, we should lay aside the feeling of threat and anxiety that attend the sexual area of our thinking. It is even proper to say that parents should give encouragement in matters of dating, sex and marriage.

It might be argued that God had the advantage of creating the perfect wife for His son. In addition, sin was not yet a figure in the equation, so perversion and aberrant behavior did not exist. Yet, notwithstanding these differences, it still could have been a threat to God to create a social force that had the potential of drawing His son away from Him. He took that risk and lays the gauntlet down for human fathers to pick up.

There are several levels at which dating skills can be taught. The first involves knowledge. Our children should hear us speak about sex, dating and marriage. In the deluge of communication avenues open to our kids, much discussion centers around sex. If they hear it properly and first from their parents, then the misinformation from the media, schoolmates and pornography will not have as much effect upon their minds. To help in this, there are scores of reliable Christian books outlining the detailed steps involved in explaining male-female relationships to children.

The second level is the example stage. The father's greatest lessons on sexuality are often taught without him even being aware of it. How a father treats his wife and daughters will go a great distance in showing his sons how to behave around women. More than anything my wife and I instruct our kids by having them copy our actions. Around the house, Kathy and I are not private about our affection for each other. We embrace often, and our kids never seem embarrassed by our public displays of affection. We tell our children that we love them dearly, but that we love each other even more. They are not threatened by this; they assume this is what marriage is supposed to be.

The third level of dating skill acquisition training is the response level. Curve balls will be thrown at our children, and they will not understand the idiosyncracies of dating simply by our prior explanations. Fathers should be on hand (and willing) to answer the thorny problems that our children will encounter when dating commences.

My own father was not terribly helpful in this matter. He only gave me one piece of advice in dating: "Don't get anyone pregnant." That left a lot to the imagination. Though I followed his advice until I was married, it was probably due more to God's grace than Dad's counsel. I have resolved to do much more than this with my children. My sons already know how their bodies work, how a girl's body works, what sex is, why it is, how it is, when it is and other pieces of knowledge.

It will be several years yet before my first boy is ready to date, but he already knows the kind of girl he wants to date. In a recent conversation about girls, he said none of the fourth-grade girls interested him. I asked him why.

"None of them are as smart or good looking as Mom," he said. That's it, son—hold out for the best! I may eventually lose a son, but in reality, I'll be gaining a "wow" for a daughter-in-law!

Spiritual Skills

Our family was at the tail end of a summer vacation. We had spent a good part of it secluded in our favorite seaside resort just north of Vancouver, British Columbia, in a little town called Sechelt. The rich primordial forests offered miles of hiking trails and hallowed mysteries to explore. Above all, I had escaped the spiritual battlefield left behind me at the office.

The second-to-last day we spent there, I felt like giving my boys a spiritual lesson. Often when we hike, I like to use nature as my own personal parable-creator. As I thought about the beauty that surrounded us, the perfect analogy came to me. John, Andrew, Ruth-Ann, Meaghan and I trudged through the fern-lined path that led down to the ocean. On a bluff overlooking a small inlet, I stopped and had them sit down around me. *Surely*, I thought, *this is how Jesus felt when He taught the crowds on the side of the mountain*. I basked in the glory of my fatherly esteem for a moment longer, then jumped into my story.

"Look out at the water, kids," I told them. "It's higher than it was last night. Do you know why?"

They thought for a second. John, who likes to be first, piped in, "I think it is because the tide is in now and it was out last night."

"Correct. And why does the tide go in and out?"

"Doesn't it have to do with the moon?" Ruth-Ann wondered.

I told her that it was indeed the result of the moon's journey around the earth. Then I asked, "Why does God have the tide go in and out?"

They looked puzzled by my riddle, so I answered it myself.

"When the tide comes in, it brings new life and vitality to the shore. When it goes out, it leaves behind living things that feed the birds and make the seashore lively and exciting." Then I applied the point of my lesson. "This is what the Bible is like for us. When we read it each day, it brings new life with it, feeding us and leaving behind the possibilities of exciting and lively times with God as our Captain. Does this make sense?"

Three heads nodded up and down. But then I noticed that Andrew had a puzzled look on his face. He is reserved, so I coaxed the question out of him.

"Come on, Andrew—what do you want to ask me?"

"Well, Dad, if reading the Bible does good stuff for you, how come you haven't read it since we left to go on vacation?" It was all I could do to breathe at that moment. His question, which came across as a rebuke, was as hard to swallow as it was accurate. In my exuberance to take time off, I had flung God's Word aside as a piece of junk mail. As we walked back to the motel, I kept thinking of an answer that would justify myself.

I couldn't think of any. There wasn't any! In my ardor to be *heard* as the spiritual foundation of the house, I was negligent in my duty to be *seen* in that role. This goes against the prime directive in all good training—*show* more than you *tell*. If I want my children to read their Bibles, I have to read mine. If I want them to pray, I must pray with them. If I want them to help the poor, they must see me reaching out with compassion to the needy.

That evening I called a family meeting. I admitted to them that I had failed in not reading my Bible. I asked their forgiveness for trying to appear spiritual when I was not. We did a group forgiving and then a group hug.

"That's My Wife's Job"

Many fathers, even those who attend church, throw off the mantle of spiritual teacher in favor of a less weighty title. They can be a football coach, homework checker and welding instructor, but when it comes to teaching children about God, they defer to their spouse: "That's my wife's department."

What is Father-God's example in this? Actually, the entire Bible is an accounting of how God taught His creation about spiritual things. Hebrews 1:1 says, "In the past God spoke to our forefathers through the prophets at many times and in various ways."

God takes every moment to pass on spiritual truth. But in case we get the erroneous idea that this is just God's job, look at Deuteronomy 6:6–9:

90

> These commandments that I give you today are
> to be upon your hearts. Impress them on your
> children. Talk about them when you sit at
> home and when you walk along the road, when
> you lie down and when you get up. Tie them as
> symbols on your hands and bind them on your
> foreheads. Write them on the doorframes of
> your houses and on your gates.

Notice how many verb-type words go into this spiritual teaching forum: impress, talk, sit, walk, lie down, get up, tie, bind and write. It is an active job. Look where it takes place: on your hearts, on your children, at home, along the road, at bedtime, on your hands, on your foreheads, doorposts, houses and gates. In a sense, God is saying, "Anytime, anyplace in any way you can, pass on what you have learned about God. Let your children know what you know."

When cancer attacked my father, he would not subject himself to the ignominies of hospital life. He wanted to be at home, sheltered in the comfort of the family he loved. Two and half months before his death, he finally met Jesus Christ the Lord. That meeting was as tempestuous as his life, and in a moment of faith, he surrendered his soul to the cleansing power of the Savior.

He was transformed that day. Mom read the Bible to him for hours at a time. When he wasn't sedated, he was hearing the Word of God and getting to know the Father he had neglected for forty years. His wilderness experience came first in his life; now he had entered the Promised Land.

Approximately three weeks before he died, he asked me to come in and talk with him. He asked many questions about my plans for the future. Then he stopped and looked me in the eye.

"Mike, please remember something."

"What, Dad?"

"It's not easy to know God. It's much easier not to know Him. It takes work to know God."

"I don't understand."

"Mike, I wasted forty years of my life not knowing God. I've learned a lot in two months because I had to."

He paused, then he said, "Mike, you don't have to waste time. Know God's Son now."

When I look at Deuteronomy 6:9, I add my own commentary to the end: "When you're dying of cancer, don't forget to teach your children."

Michael Phillips, and his wife, Kathy, have four children. A career pastor, he asks only that you not call him "Reverend."

Busy Hands Are Frantic Hands

taken from
*I Hate Whining Except
When I'm Doing It*

by Sheila Rabe

I went past the field of the sluggard,
  past the vineyard of the man who lacks
    judgment;
thorns had come up everywhere,
  the ground was covered with weeds,
  and the stone wall was in ruins.
I applied my heart to what I observed
  and learned a lesson from what I saw:
A little sleep, a little slumber,
  a little folding of the hands to rest—
and poverty will come on you like a bandit
  and scarcity like an armed man.

(Proverbs 24:30-34)

Apples simmered on the stove. Clean jars lined the counter, waiting to be filled with applesauce. Three large boxes of apples sat on the kitchen floor. I stood amid this mess, washing, cutting, stirring.

Junior, in the toddler stage, was "helping." He was so busy! He would take an apple from one box and deliver it to another. Then he would remove an apple from that second box and put it in yet another box.

I chuckled and thought, *Isn't that cute? He's so busy. And in his baby mind he thinks he is doing something important. Funny. He reminds me of someone I know. . . .*

That someone was me, running from activity to activity. A PTO meeting here, a committee meeting there. Now it's time for my writing class. Tomorrow night is church choir practice after I have two afternoon appointments. Saturday is my songwriter's critique group. Yesterday I said I'd help plan the Welcome Wagon's annual spring luncheon and style show. . . .

Busy hands are happy hands, right? Then let's get a little happier. Run here, run there. See me running everywhere.

One day I found I'd run out of breath and couldn't do all those important things. Suddenly I wasn't happy any more. And neither was my family.

The kids knew they had a mother. Their father fondly remembered her. "Yes, she had brown hair. Nice eyes, too. She was fun. There she goes, children, driving down the street. I think she's off to. . . . Let me check. It's Wednesday. She's gone to choir practice."

After that sighting the kids began to look for Mom. Other Mommy sightings were reported but could not be confirmed—by the time a child dragged someone to the spot where Mom had been seen, she had rushed somewhere else. "I tell you, I saw her. Right there. Loading clothes in the dryer."

"How do you know it was her? Did you see her face?"

"No. But I recognized her voice when she said, 'Not now, I'm busy.' She was here, I tell you!"

I kept running faster, finding more things to do—all of them important. A friend told me to slow down and cut some things out of my life.

"I can't cut out anything," I insisted. "Everything I'm doing is important."

He looked like he didn't believe me.

I believed me. Until I got sick. Not the kind of sick where my family feared for my life, just sick enough to be couch-bound for a couple of weeks.

Once down, I looked around me. I saw my friend, Vonda, a high-energy, multitalented overachiever, suddenly drop everything and go to a health farm to rest for three weeks. Another friend complained that stress was killing her. One friend bragged about her crazy schedule. Did I ever brag? Come to think of it, I did.

I remembered the two New Testament sisters, Mary and Martha. Contemplating Christ's words to Martha in Luke 10:41-42, I decided I spent much time on second-rate things.

Why? Probably for the same reason Martha fussed over the dinner for Jesus. Probably for the same reason my friend bragged about her full schedule. I wanted to be important and needed. And anyway, so many things needed attention. Who could do them better than I could?

Honestly, nearly anyone would have been better at some of those things. Atilla the Hun's mother would have made a more patient school health room volunteer. ("You're not sick. Go back to class!") And my lack of organizational skills hardly qualified me to be secretary in a women's club. ("I'd love to read the minutes from last month's meeting, but I can't find them")

Then there was the time I directed "German Day" at the small German church where my husband and I served. I was full of ideas. But by the end of the celebration, several members of the church board probably had some ideas too—about what they'd like to do to me!

Entertainment for "German Day" was the first disaster. I got a painful case of telephone ear trying to find a German oompah band. Unfortunately, every oompah band from here to Munich was booked for that day.

"OK, the oompah band is out, but I've got a line on a great husband-and-wife duo!" I said. The duo idea failed. Next we were down to a strolling accordian player who canceled at the last minute. We played records.

Publicity was another challenge. When I put the wrong date in the paper, I encountered the Christian equivalent of a lynch mob, ready to string me up. Our event was Saturday, but the paper announced Sunday. "Look on the bright side," I said with a weak smile. "We'll have lots of visitors for church." No one was amused.

How did I get sucked into these activities in the first place? Simple. Volunteers are a dying breed. Organizations beat the bushes for them, and when they find one, they throw a net of flattery over the unsuspecting prey. "You'd be perfect," they purr.

The poor, foolish person believes them. For a while. Until she sees a similarity between a toddler with an apple and herself.

Learning to discern between busyness and business is difficult to do. I suspect we must all make our share of mistakes before we can accurately know our capabilities and limitations.

Only in the past two or three years have I been able to assess my abilities and limits accurately. Because I have a strong personality and lots of ideas and enthusiasm, I often am mistaken for a leader. But good leaders are organized and can delegate and follow through. And they have persistence.

I don't. I'm a sprinter, not a distance runner. I don't readily hang in there for the long haul. I lose my enthusiasm and shlep through my job, biding my time, waiting for the end. Short projects work best for me.

Since learning this, it's easier for me to turn down flattering offers for long-term offices. I am better at spearheading committees or simply brainstorming.

Since I have limited time to spend on causes beyond my home and church, I'm learning to consider my strengths when needs and opportunities waltz by. Before getting bamboozled into anything, I ask myself, *Does this use my greatest skills? If not, does God want to build this skill in me? Or is someone better qualified to do it?*

I'm facing a new school year, but I've already decided those volunteer hunters will never take me alive. The middle school PTO needed a treasurer. "Who would like to do this?" the president pleaded.

The principal said, "I hear Mrs. Rabe is good with money."

He's talking about the woman who tried to balance the family checkbook once and put the family a thousand dollars in the hole. No. Mrs. Rabe is not good with money. Mrs. Rabe will not hold a PTO office next year. Nor will she be at the health room. And she probably won't even direct publicity for the school carnival.

That does not mean I won't do anything. But I will do less. I'll use my particular talents where I really am needed—not where I'd like to think I'm needed.

Ecclesiastes 3:1 says there is a season for everything. I've finally realized that seasons follow one another. They don't come simultaneously. My mother says we do different things at different times in our lives. I used to agree with this outwardly, but secretly thought I could be different. Now I know I can't.

Over the years I've also learned that not every season is a time of frantic activity. Fall is a season of winding down, and winter is one of quiet and rest, of death before resurrection. Plants and trees take a snooze and gather strength for the coming spring.

We all need a season of rest to renew our strength. We need time to hibernate, to let our bodies gather new strength for the work ahead. The body that never pauses, stops. Forever.

Rest is wonderful. In fact, it's so beneficial that God designed one day a week simply to ensure our rest. At that time, we're to follow the example of the one who created us (Genesis 2:2). As we follow His example and turn our thoughts toward Him, we renew ourselves for the next season of activity.

Too many times in the past my day of rest was busier than the other six. In addition to all the church activities and undone Saturday chores loomed SUNDAY DINNER, a ritual invented for all the Marthas of the world. Sunday dinner was always impressive and often involved company.

Maybe that's why Sunday dinner was impressive. The family doesn't need impressing. But company . . . !

Entertaining, for many of us, can be an ego thing. We want to fascinate our friends with our culinary skills, our lovely table setting, our general creativeness. So we cook, bake, scrub and clean ourselves into exhaustion—for a few "oohs" and "aahs."

Sometimes we knock ourselves out because of worry born of a lack of self-esteem. If I don't produce an outstanding meal, my friends will be disappointed. They'll think we don't consider them important. They'll scorn my cooking. They'll never come back. I fret.

It doesn't work that way. When was the last time you scorned something someone else cooked? I've discovered most people will happily eat anything they don't have to prepare. They appreciate any effort to give the chef a day off. Besides, our friends don't come to our homes for a free meal. They come to see us, to laugh, to be encouraged. They come for fellowship, not fancy food.

Now our Sunday dinner is easy—hot dogs, hamburgers, soup and bread. If we entertain, the fare is still simple. Sometimes we potluck with friends, everyone contributing so no one must do much. Rest, I am learning, is wonderful.

One family I know gives its mom a day of rest by preparing the meal once a week. Mom can relax while Dad and the boys prepare Sunday dinner. Imagine that—Mother's Day every week!

Even an entire day of rest isn't enough when the other six are packed with feverish activity. No one can "do it all."

Ignore newspaper and magazine articles about spectacular overachievers. Those tales highlight the achievements of a person—the area the individual has poured precious time, talent and energy into. The articles usually don't mention the unfinished chores, neglected talents, lost "opportunites" for service, sacrifices or damaged health. And they certainly don't highlight the failures, broken families or poor relationships with children.

I wish they did. Maybe then we would see that a runner can't win a footrace by trying to jump broad jumps at the same time. He can't get the breath he needs to run if he's singing the national anthem while trotting around the track.

One goal at a time is enough for anyone. The myth of the superwoman who balances family, brilliant career and community service is dead. Many of us need to stop trying to give the poor creature CPR.

I can't afford to go to a health resort for three weeks, so I've decided to become less important. My calendar will have days with nothing written on them. I'll avoid the net of flattery and use my few talents where they're most needed. Instead of covering every base, I'll play one position well and let God find team members for the other positions. I'll stand still long enough for my children to see me and know me.

No more rushing from box to box, shuffling apples. I want to make applesauce—not a mess.

Sheila Rabe is a popular romance writer with thirteen books to her credit plus two other books, *I Hate Whining . . . Except When I'm Doing It* and *It's a Wonderful (Mid)Life!* A wife and mother, Sheila is also active in various ministries in her local church.

Values That Form Us

taken from
Finishing Well

by Mark Lee

In his book *Hide or Seek,* James Dobson summarized the life of Lee Harvey Oswald, assassin of President John F. Kennedy in Dallas, Texas in 1963. He described the tragic Oswald as an unlovely, unloved, incorrigible, lonely man, who failed in virtually everything he ever tried except for rifle marksmanship. He won infamy by using his single skill to murder the President of the United States. Dobson attributed Oswald's moral failure in part to being reared in a life context largely devoid of standard values that build character, esteem and family.

The matter of values, especially Christian values, and how to generate them in practical conduct is the focus of this chapter. Christian values contrast sharply with the values society maintains, so we must learn to differentiate.

Every culture has its own set of values which it may analyze in terms of continuums. There may be a continuum that has beauty at one end and ugliness at the other, genius at one extreme and retardation at the other or various continuums of values deemed important by that society. In *Hide or Seek,* Dobson reviewed two of the popular values in America: beauty and intelligence. Beauty he labeled the "gold coin" of American values, and intelligence he called the "silver coin."

The Coin of Beauty

In his analysis, Dobson suggested that members of the population, even inadvertently sometimes, are aware of the continuum of beauty and ugliness, and would wish to believe themselves beautiful. The same applies to intelligence. It is interesting to note that in a 1992 Harris Poll conducted for the March of Dimes, respondents gave their highest approval for genetic experiments aimed at improving a child's physical characteristics (forty-three percent), with improving intelligence coming in right behind (forty-two percent).[1] Interestingly, the matter of improving morality was not addressed.

A distorted view of beauty may begin early in life when children inadvertently allow the messages of the classic nursery rhymes and children's stories to shape their feelings and thoughts about beauty. Consider some of these familiar titles: "The Ugly Duckling," "Rudolph, the Red-Nosed Reindeer," "Cinderella," "Snow White," "Dumbo the Flying Elephant" and "Sleeping Beauty." Sleeping Beauty, for example, remains beautiful after ninety-nine years of sleep and can only be awakened by the kiss of a handsome prince. He has to be handsome.

There are many similar stories, and they generally teach that being beautiful is being good or having authority and power. Ugliness, on the other hand, equates with badness, sadness, menial treatment, even death. The implication: homely persons are not good. And life experience seems to bear out this distortion of values.

Before they are very old, children learn the importance adults place on beauty. The most attractive children tend to get the best grades in school. They are treated with kinder words and greater acceptance than less attractive children. If a child is "bad," he may believe himself to be ugly, or, believing himself to be ugly, he may decide he is also bad. He may ultimately believe he is his group's "ugly duckling." The illusion of ugly/bad or bad/ugly extends to later years. Research in the field shows that prison inmates by and large do not perceive themselves to be physically attractive.

Many years ago, in a home for orphans, I watched the way in which every Friday the children were presented to prospective adoptive parents. The children would walk through a room where they were observed for consideration. A blond, blue-eyed little girl walked through just once and was adopted. But a lad with the strawberry mark down the side of his face was never spoken for. Such is society's focus on beauty. The less-than-perfect child who needed parents most was not chosen. That lad was a candidate for future antisocial behavior.

The Coin of Intelligence

Dobson's silver coin is intelligence. Parents commonly speak of their children as being precocious, well above average. The parents seem to place greater value on children they perceive to be highly intelligent than on those of supposed lesser intelligence. Intelligence is so important to parents that average children are now perceived by their parents to be near genius. Evaluation is distorted. We are told that "grade inflation" takes place in colleges and universities because so many "must" get high grades—whether earned or not.

When I was teaching I noticed how parents in general perceived their children as gifted, whether or not they had any grounds for such evaluation. When parents brought their college-bound youths to campus early in September, they met faculty members at a reception which was part of the orientation activities. As their embarrassed son or daughter stood by, they extolled his or her potential, though they sometimes admitted that the young person's high school scholarship and discipline might not warrant such an evaluation. If the student records did not prove the parents' high view of his or her ability, there was always an excuse: The high school was not as efficient as it should have been; the teachers were not dedicated; the courses were boring. Evidence shows, however, that in general, poor performance was more likely due to home influences that permitted excessive television viewing or other distractions—anything from family feuds to interminable loud music or even free use of an automobile. (Several studies show direct correlation of the free use of vehicles to reduction in academic performance.)

In many of these homes, too, family activity included virtually nothing in terms of relevant reading or meaningful discussion. A boy will not easily believe that reading is highly beneficial to his life if he never observes his father reading a substantive book or even an article from a first-rate periodical. Father implies, even if he does not state the case, that he is successful and adjusted in life. Why should the son, to match father's accomplishments, do what his father does not do?

Raw intelligence is not nearly so important as what one does with it, regardless of the importance society places on grades and test scores. Sometimes no amount of effort will result in academic success. When a child does not accomplish what families with high achievement traditions expect, tension and disappointment among family members may arise. Often that disappointment seems to them justified, even when a problem like retardation is the cause. Many of these families seem to feel that the family's reputation has been diminished or tarnished in some way. Their focus is not on maturity related to circumstances, but rather on family pride.

Certainly society does place stress on beauty and intelligence, but at least one more coin should be added to Dobson's collection—the coin of materialism. Every culture has its own range of wealth and poverty. In American culture, and only slightly less in Canadian, materialism dominates much of life.

The Coin of Materialism

When certain persons enter a room, they instantly convey an image of their wealth or influence (or of the illusions of these qualities). These impressive men and women are afforded privilege. People are drawn to wealth. Even in families, members divide between rich uncles and poor ones. An individual is treated a certain way by other family members based on the way they view his financial standing in relation to their own. Poor relatives place expectations on rich ones, expectations that often go far beyond the actual powers of their wealth or influence.

Nearly everything in the English-speaking world, especially the United States, is evaluated in the terms of dollars. Refugees often remark that the country they left emphasized homely values, while their new country, the United States, seems to them to have only one value—materialism. Many refugees say they would be pleased to be back in their own country if power politics and abject poverty did not prevent their return. They do not believe that improved living standards are fair exchange for life qualities. They feel they have no choice.

Emerging generations believe that wealth should be self-perpetuating. Although the first generation may have to make great sacrifices to achieve a degree of prosperity, the second generation does not have to work so hard. Still, the second generation often holds on to the values they admired in their parents. The third or fourth generation often loses the early perception of values attached to prosperity. They seem to think that one is entitled to the good life simply because he is an American or Canadian and alive. The work ethic is diluted, but expectations remain high and may even go higher.

Populations everywhere want what money can buy. Most persons work for money, but many hope for inheritances and windfalls along the way. Some hope to get money from begging, gambling or from crimes ranging from thievery to tax evasion. Theft is common, touching the majority of families in one way or another. Or, the love of money can lead to major crimes of embezzlement, drug running, piracy or even murder for profit.

Although our culture seems to think that wealth is everything, what or how much one owns is not really the issue. The issues are: 1) the attitude one holds toward wealth and its priority in things, and 2) the stewardship of material wealth, since wealth can be an effective tool for service. Affluent persons are not put down in the Scriptures, but they are called to use their possessions generously and to minister. Both the rich and the poor can be faithful in the use of their material goods—much or little.

Christian Values

In Second Peter 1:3-11 the apostle Peter lists eight values related to Christian thought and practice. He writes that when we make these priorities in regular practice, we may expect remarkable results. The values he lists are faith, virtue, knowledge, temperance, patience, godliness, brotherly kindness and love. He did not imply that the list is exhaustive, but he did propose enough to keep serious Christians busy.

Each of these values could be seen as a continuum. A continuum places opposite values at each end of a line, permitting those who use the scale to judge approximate percentages for each position along the way. No one can measure accurately these percentages as they relate to human behavior—only God can measure such a matter. But the continuum provides a tool to show individuals the degree to which they may possess certain positive or negative qualities. When used, it gives an important point of reference. "Each one should test his own actions. Then he can take pride in himself, without comparing himself to somebody else" (Galatians 6:4).

Faith

There is a continuum of faith and unbelief.

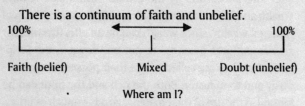

Faith (belief)   Mixed   Doubt (unbelief)

Where am I?

When we analyze our faith, we will often find that some doubt remains, at least related to some issues. The existence of some doubt, as Augustine taught, does not mean we are devoid of spiritual life effectiveness. But it does mean that to the degree that doubt exists, we are not functioning at the spiritual level we might be. By generating greater faith, a Christian improves his confidence and demonstrates a more effective spiritual life. The maturing Christian will sense fulfillment as he moves away from doubt and toward total belief.

The apostle Peter clearly desired that his readers improve themselves in the direction of the values he listed. He began the listing with faith. Faith, as discussed earlier, is vital for all Christians. It is the end of the continuum toward which the mature Christian is consciously moving.

Righteousness

There is a continuum of righteousness and evil.

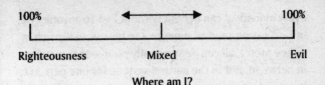

100%   100%

Righteousness   Mixed   Evil

Where am I?

Those persons practicing Christian virtue are concerned with righteousness, fidelity, honesty, duty, responsibility and mercy. Those with less virtue will display, to some degree, infidelity, dishonesty, disrespect of duty, disregard of responsibility and lack of mercy. We are addressing here Christian righteousness. Other religions may advance what they call virtue but what in Christianity is evil. For example, the murder of neighbors who are infidels may be a virtue in some religions. In Christianity, however, the murder of any person is evil.

From the apostle Peter's first letter, we learn that Christians who progress toward the righteousness end of the continuum may, by their worthy conduct, draw attention to the good in life (1 Peter 3:13-17). Peter implied that every Christian may find and practice these values, if he chooses to do so. Virtue is not limited to specially gifted or highly educated Christians. The simplest person, if he is a Christian, may practice virtues that equal or surpass those of a genius who is also a Christian. The simple Christian may accept straightforwardly the Christian way, while the intellectual may be tempted to dilute biblical injunctions or redefine them, modifying virtue to his own preferences.

The Christian system of values stands in contrast to other systems of values in that in the Christian system, every individual can benefit without loss to anyone else. In God's economy, all persons can be spiritually rich or, if they prefer, all can be spiritually poor—or somewhere in between. But in the natural system, for one person to be enriched, another may become impoverished. No matter how gifted or talented the population may be, some persons will be rich, and some will be poor.

Mature persons will resist the urge to measure themselves by society's values. Instead, they will seek the values that emanate from God. These are enriching, satisfying values, available to any and all who seek spiritually valued tender. With that exchange, persons may enrich those around them and impoverish no one.

Knowledge

There is also a continuum of knowledge and ignorance.

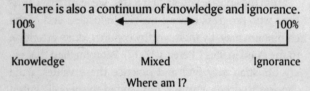

Where am I?

While society places high value on intelligence, spiritual knowledge is of major importance to the maturing Christian. Infants are born with a degree of intelligence, but they are not born with anything more than prenatal knowledge. As far as knowledge is concerned, we all start at the same place—we are all born in relative ignorance. But as infants mature, they increase in knowledge which helps them to function well in their world. And as Christians mature, they should be growing in knowledge that helps them to function well in their spiritual lives. This knowledge is largely gained from a study of the Bible, which provides a solid, logical basis upon which persons may pattern their beliefs and conduct.

Action is key. Only as a person applies knowledge can he gain more. When knowledge, whether spiritual or natural, is acted upon favorably, more knowledge presents itself as surely as a second mile becomes possible only to those who traverse the first. Steps cannot be skipped, but some participants are more swift than others in covering the necessary distance.

Ignorance, at one end of the spectrum, is among the most knotty of man's problems. Ignorance prevents him from solving problems. The worst kind of ignorance is that of pride, which pits human knowledge against God's. But there is also human laziness that results in apathetic attitudes toward spiritual growth or even intellectual growth. Such laziness avoids searching for God. But mature persons seek knowledge and adjust their conduct to what they find. The Scripture refers to spiritual knowledge as "true knowledge."

Temperance

There is a continuum of temperance and license.

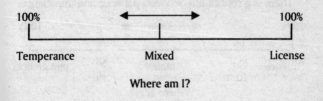

Where am I?

The opposite end of the continuum from license is not total self-denial, but temperance. Temperance is the balance between all and none. When we are moderate, we avoid overusing or underusing what is available. Temperance enjoys creation without abusing it or ourselves.

License, on the negative side, is displayed in drunkenness, gluttony, in the excess of anything, even religion. Religiosity is a kind of intemperance, a distortion. The Scriptures warn about the matter even in reference to prayer. We are warned to avoid "babbling like pagans, [who] think they will be heard because of their many words" (Matthew 6:7).

Intemperance commonly becomes the norm. Some erroneously use statistical averages to discover the temperate life, not realizing these averages are often already skewed toward license. A national average for body weights, for example, was formerly determined by the weight of all divided by the number of subjects questioned. If the general population tends toward gluttony, then the average may well be evidence of intemperance, and therefore a poor guideline by which to judge body weight. The mature person must become master of his own temperance.

Patience

There is a continuum between patience and impatience.

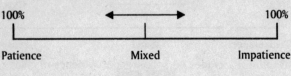

Where am I?

Patience in a person is evidence of self-control. Impatient persons too readily react to conduct of others that does not mesh with their own. Because so much conduct in others does not synchronize with ours, we can quickly test our level of patience.

Patience is expected from persons who are mature, as we expect it from parents interacting with their children. Patient persons act "grown up." They are aware that the immediate event is not the end of things. Matters will be better tomorrow or next week. There is no need to overreact. It will take years to form the infant into a boy, the boy into an adolescent, the adolescent into an adult and the adult into a mature person. Patient men and women tend to become more aware of the wholeness of life and are inclined to problem-solving.

Those who are impatient are often lacking in other values like faith and self-control. They tend to react to problems rather than solve them. Impatience marks the child; patience the mature adult.

Godliness

There is a continuum of godliness and ungodliness.

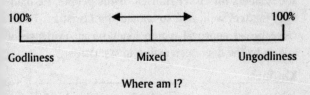

Godliness includes personal virtue, evidence of characteristics related to Christlikeness. It begins with an awareness of God that leads to awe and worship. The godly person makes an effort to live righteously, evading carnal thought and conduct. Even so, the concern here is not so much with good and evil, but with personal character which reflects, even relates to, God's character.

Ungodliness centers in rebellion against God. It ranges from a neglect of God and His preferences to a kind of ferocity in some persons who do not believe in God but are angry at Him for "not existing." Even references to God trigger ill feelings in them, perhaps venomous reactions. Prayer is disdained; every church is a leech on society. This is a common public response in some atheistic movements. Their activism has generated legislation favorable to their views. Some are almost violent when discussing a God they perceive as too unloving or powerless to intervene in situations they believe are tragic to mankind. They may even lash out against general, legitimate conduct, accepted as appropriate in a free society.

No negative response should deter genuine Christian conduct and belief, even when such activity creates enemies. Even God does not expect approval from all men and women, for either Himself or His people. He manages matters well, and so should the Christian. To receive broad approval would likely be an evidence of failure by the devout to maintain standards.

Kindness

There is a continuum of kindness and unkindness.

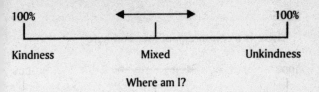

100%   100%

Kindness   Mixed   Unkindness

Where am I?

A kind person accepts others whether they are wrong, weak, noisy, ignorant or whatever. Kind persons never wish to see anyone excluded simply for personal reasons. Kind men and women are safe to be around. We can reveal ourselves without the fear of ostracism. Kindness, we readily sense, is a sign of maturity. We see it in its simplest form when an adult works patiently with a boisterous, slow-to-learn or fearful child.

Unkind persons, on the other hand, prefer to have weak, wrong or unlikeable people out of the way. Unkind men and women, even children, are not safe to be around. There is nothing in the unkind person to inspire. There is little or no reciprocity or fairness. If logical they would be kind if for no better reason than that they will need kindness for themselves in the future. The unkind person often takes without giving back.

Job, characterized frequently for his patience, was also a kind person, as demonstrated by his concern for the slave, the poor, the widow, the orphan, the ill-clothed, the hungry, the accused, the innocent, the stranger. He did not so much as speak ill of an avowed enemy (Job 31:29-30). He was understandably perplexed, then, when his friends did not act kindly toward him in his sufferings. But like Job, the mature believer will be kind to others even when that kindness is not returned.

Love

There is a continuum of love and hate.

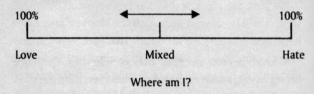

100%		100%
Love	Mixed	Hate

Where am I?

Loving persons are special blessings. Any family with loving persons among its members is greatly blessed. The loving person is pleasing to be around because he controls his will in order to act and believe in unselfish and Christlike ways.

The love Peter indicated in this text is not the love that is so familiar in the current culture. "In love" romance is ephemeral, dissolving when one member or the other fails in a relationship. The Greek word *agape* used often in the Scriptures finds its meaning in the unselfish nature of the lover, not in the object of that unconditional love. Another Greek word for love, *eros* relates to human passion. *Eros*, in its original meaning, was noble for its purpose, but is too narrow for mature love. *Eros* finds its attraction in the love object, not in the character of the lover.

Even the Greek word *phileo*, which implies a natural and useful kind of reciprocal love, is too narrow. The apostle Peter was writing about *agape* love in this context—defined in First Corinthians 13. Such love is mature, shining upon and blessing all who share in the life of the loving person. In a population strong with self in-terest, this kind of love is in short supply.

Because the topic of love has been treated often and well, it will be passed over with the few remarks made here. But let there be no doubt that love is indispens-able to maturity. Even society in general relates love to maturity, as suggested by the results of a study reported in *Psychology Today:* "We found that when parents—par-ticularly mothers—really loved their children, the sons and daughters were likely to achieve the highest levels of social and moral maturity."[2] How much more impor-tant is love to the development of Christian maturity.

Hate is the opposite of love. It too becomes an attitude that persists in the will. It is bitter, destructive, evil and holds in it no promise of good for anyone. Nevertheless, people—some abandoned wives or husbands, for exam-ple—do sometimes turn to it, hoping to find solace. But hatred, often carried out in revenge, offers only false hope for peace. Hatred always results in bitterness, which becomes its own punishment. Hatred degrades the bitter person who clings to it as though it were the only satisfac-tion available. Love, on the other hand, uplifts not only the lover, but also the one who is loved. And it leads to maturity among those who practice it.

We have briefly reviewed the eight values Peter out-lined as essential to mature Christian living. At this point some may find that the idea of Christian maturity seems too difficult. For others, it may seem too complex. It is neither, although it is true that personal development is hard work—it is extensive and time-consuming. The fea-tures of maturity are clear enough, and every Christian has the assistance of the Holy Spirit to make them achievable. It is very important—and cannot be overemphasized—that even a small increment in improvement makes a large difference.

The mature Christian will cultivate the values Peter listed in combination to make up a gracious spiritual life. But to simplify matters, it is helpful to consider each of the values separately. The Christian who finds himself well along in some factors, partially along in others and barely begun in still others needs to devote himself to those features nagging for attention. A Christian strong in faith, but short on kindness, ought to give serious attention to the cultivation of kindness. Strong in temperance, he may need help in developing patience. Each person should make his own diagnosis and then proceed by prescribing improvements for himself, learning from both successful and unsuccessful experiences, from models and biblical concepts. Such a person is headed toward maturity.

The P.A.C.E. Principles

In the context of values there are patterns of conduct which turn into habits and move the Christian in the right direction on the various continua. These patterns can become a way of life. Cast in an acrostic, they make up the P.A.C.E. principles: Prayer, Acceptance, Communication and Example. Each is divided into two parts and, when applied, can serve well in one's search for personal, Christian maturity. The following presents something of a summary of their personal applications in my observation of experience and personal life.

Prayer

Prayer can be divided into two kinds—public and private—but even church members do not give much thought to either, especially private prayer. For many churchgoers, prayer is perceived as something that the pastor does at some point in the church service. Public prayer, then, is sincere, worshipful, general, and it usually follows a formula of address, adoration, confession, assurance, petition, hope and benediction. Some church members seem satisfied that they have all the prayer they need if they hear the pastoral prayer on Sundays and recite a paragraph for grace at mealtimes—tossing in the Lord's Prayer on formal occasions or as a substitute for personal prayer.

In his book *Christian Maturity,* E. Stanley Jones said that this is not enough. Jones challenged Christians to regular, personal prayer because as he traveled and talked to Christians from many different backgrounds and cultures, he found that the "greatest source of weakness in character and influence is to be found in the prayer life." He believed that most of "the casualties in the spiritual life" are related to weakened prayer activity. "Prayer is pivotal," he affirmed.

Jones observed a direct correlation between his personal quality of life and the amount of time he spent in prayer. When he was prayerful, he said he felt like an illuminated lightbulb fixed firmly in its socket. But when he lacked prayer, he said he felt like a lightbulb pulled out of its socket. For Jones, a person is no more likely to be vital spiritually without prayer than a lightbulb is to produce light without being connected to its energy source.

Private prayer addresses personal needs and is therefore more individual than public prayer. The most effective prayer I ever remember praying was a simple two words: "Oh, God." I repeated them numerous times over the space of a number of minutes. They flowed up from deep inside me like hot, heavy lava. If others had been present, they probably would not have been comfortable listening to my prayer, but I was not praying for others. I was praying to God and only to God. And God heard and answered that simple, heartfelt prayer, providing me with peace and comfort.

Prayer may have broader uses than most persons imagine. On one occasion I was so angered by the unsatisfactory conduct of one of my children that when he later made strong protest to me, I asked him to pray for me. I told him I felt ill will toward him and was angry at his attitude. After additional protest, he acquiesced. Before continuing long into the prayer, he was praying for himself. The experience changed him in dramatic ways, perhaps changed me as well. Civility never was lost in our exchanges thereafter.

For the mature Christian, prayer—especially brief, private prayers expressed throughout the day—becomes a way of life. Anything in his life can be immediately, sincerely and intensely (or casually, depending on circumstances) touched by prayer. He is prayerful about family relationships, a trip in his car, an ache in his back or whatever else may be on his mind. He freely prays in the night when he awakens and sleep eludes him. There is a kind of prayerful trust that is as common to him as the air he breathes.

Acceptance

Acceptance has two facets: self-acceptance and acceptance of others. But the acceptance of others is related to self-acceptance. If a person cannot accept himself, he will have distorted, often excessively high expectations of others, yet he holds himself in reserve to avoid the possibility or illusion of failure. Relationships commonly warp because of distorted perceptions of self and others.

A person's age, body size, geographic location, profession, competence, health, education and faith—all may factor into one's degree of self-acceptance. Within boundaries, we must learn to like who we are, not wishing to be someone else.

At the close of a summer conference, a lady asked for counsel. When she and her husband arrived at our cabin, my wife offered them seats on the couch. The woman took the extreme end to the left, her husband sat far right, leaving a space between them that seemed like a canyon. My wife and I sat on chairs opposite the couple.

"He won't let me have a nose job," the woman said hooking her thumb toward her husband. "And he can afford it."

"You wish to have plastic surgery on your nose?" I asked.

"Yes, an eighth of an inch off the end of my nose."

Turning to her husband, I asked his opinion.

"She is the most beautiful woman I have ever seen. I like her just the way she is, and so do the children," he said. "This thing is hurting our family. I don't want her to do it, and the children don't like it either. This whole thing focuses too much on a matter unsuitable to what we stand for. There is too much accent on a body and face. God gave her what she's got."

I asked the woman if she had any other problems.

"My thighs are too thick," she retorted.

I determined not to talk about that, so I went back to discussing her nose. "Give me your right profile," I requested.

She turned her face slightly left. I repeated the request for the opposite profile. My wife and I both noticed that the woman was quite attractive and exuded a picture of good health. While cosmetic surgery might well be indicated for some persons, especially for those disfigured in some way, strong objections to such surgery from loving family members might mean that the person was putting too much emphasis in some areas and too little in others.

For this woman, the higher Christian values were not in place. She was immature. Her desire to be "someone else" prevented her from gaining self-acceptance and denied easy acceptance of her by her husband and children.

Communication

Communication also involves two kinds: sending and receiving. One depends on the other. But while there appears to be no lack of senders, listening appears to be a weak art in interpersonal relationships. The mature person will work to master effective listening skills. In so doing he will serve both himself and others.

One of the most poignant stories I ever heard was told by my wife about an incident that happened to her when she was in junior high school. One day was dark for some particular reason—an injustice long since forgotten. Perhaps a boy pulled her curls, a teacher misunderstood her conduct or a test did not go as well as expected. Whatever the cause, my wife tried to tell her mother about the event. But her mother moved from room to room as though escaping her daughter's incessant conversation. She pursued, and her mother, still on the move, responded, "Uh huh," "Yeah," "Am-m-m," "Hm-m-m," "Yeah," "Uh-huh."

At last the daughter stopped, stood in the center of the living room and silently screamed, addressing her mother in her thoughts: "I will not tell you anything that means anything to me as long as I live." And she did not, until many years later.

Sometimes a person feels that he must talk, so he simply talks. The mature person will not mind listening, and when the first person has said what he or she wishes to say, the listener, because he has listened well, will be able to respond meaningfully. He will better understand the facts and feelings of the other person because he has heard them fully. Such communication creates fewer opportunities for misunderstanding, error and offense. The listener will be wiser, and he will speak to persons who respect what he has to say because he has first listened to them. The mature listener tends to cultivate four skills: greeting (recognizing the speaker), healing (considering the emotional state of the speaker), finding (discovering the relevant facts) and evaluating (suggesting what needs to follow). Effective communication is a mark of the mature person.

Example

Example is of two kinds: biblical and personal. Personal example, or modeling, is well-known. Even though a Christian principle, it is also universal among civilizations. Pagan tribes expect tribal members to model their values, just as teachers in ancient Greece and Rome made modeling a major feature of family and formal education. It was vital in the law of Israel, and remains in Christian teachings. Moses instructed the Israelites to teach their children by example, and Paul urged believers to follow him in the way he followed Christ.

The principle is basic: if we want to teach our children to avoid lying, we must not lie. If we want them to refrain from stealing, we also refrain from stealing. Positive values are taught in affirmative modeling. We teach the value of work by working, the value of kindness by being kind and the value of giving by giving ourselves and gifts to others.

Mature people both lead and follow. Both are done best by those who believe in modeling. Effective following is vital to effective leading. Maturing Christians find examples in other mature Christians, and they find examples from the Scriptures. Some biblical examples are affirmative (Joseph, Abigail, Nehemiah, Paul) and some negative (Ahab, Herod, Demas). Either way, these biblical characters provide valuable models for cultivating maturity.

When daughters-in-law were added to our family, I knew that I wanted to gain rapport, show love and encourage family solidarity with them. I did what I had done before in situations where I wanted an example to follow—I went to the Scriptures. In the past I had found models there for marriage, ministry, friendship, stewardship, parenting and what have you. Surely there would be a model for fathers-in-law.

For my in-law father lesson, I found Jethro, father-in-law to Moses. He seems to have been as nearly perfect a father and father-in-law one may find. Admittedly the narrative is sketchy, but there is enough of the story for the purpose. From that story, one finds that Jethro's treatment of Moses could not be much improved upon. He did many positive things including the reconciliation of Moses with Zipporah. He offered wise counsel for the governing of God's people in the wilderness. Jethro appeared ready to assist wherever he could and was unwilling to become a burden to anyone.

With Jethro in mind, I determined to do what I could to develop good relationships with our children's mates. I found myself speculating about what Jethro might have done in modern circumstances. I felt he would have done whatever he could to keep child and spouse together. He would not have interfered, but he would have been available. He would have assisted when matters became difficult, if assistance was appropriate. He would have been friendly and objectively concerned. But he would have bowed out when his participation was no longer needed.

With such lessons from Jethro, I occupied myself to become an acceptable father-in-law.

Putting into practice what I was learning, I took my daughter-in-law out to lunch one afternoon. We talked the whole time about her husband, my son. After lunch I asked her if she was in a hurry to be someplace and since she was not, I took her to a mall and bought her a pantsuit that I knew she wanted.

"There," I said. "Go home and model that for your husband, and say, 'This is what your dad purchased for me; now what do you have to offer?' " We laughed, and I took her home. That was the first of many other enjoyable exchanges, thanks to Jethro.

Scripture provides the models for all those who desire to grow to spiritual maturity. It provides examples for specific areas of Christian conduct and, in its implications, is also useful for creating a "big picture" for Christian living.

Endnotes

1. *USA Today*, September 29, 1992, sec. A, p. 13.
2. David C. McClelland, et al., "Making It to Maturity," *Psychology Today*, June 1978, p. 45.

Mark Lee is the author of more than a dozen books on family, parenting, leadership and ministry issues. His long and fruitful career has encompassed several stages, including communication management consultation, conference ministries and college professor, president and chancellor.

CHAPTER 10

Speaking Childese— Fathers and Communication

taken from
To Be a Father Like the Father

by Michael Phillips

Parents are capable of communicating well, especially to each other. Ditto for children; they can communicate effectively to others their age. Yet when parents and their children try to speak to one another, it sometimes becomes a messy and even brutal exchange.

I have often wondered why this has to be, and lately, I have come up with a theory. One day my preschool daughter was left at home with me, her sagacious and lazy father, while her mother went shopping. I felt I was entitled to laziness on this Monday, the pastor's perennial day off.

Picture my daughter: braids, beautiful dimples when she smiles, very petite with only twenty-five pounds of power in her small frame. *I can handle this one*, I thought as I lounged in front of the television watching a sports program. Little did I realize that my tranquil day was about to be annihilated by my sweet little girl.

Events unfolded innocently enough. "Daddy," she said, batting her eyelashes, "can I have something to eat?"

"What would you like, sweetheart?" I asked, forgetting that parents should never give their children multiple choices.

"I want a bag of M&Ms."

At this point it dawned on me that my daughter had just recently completed lunch and that my wife had said she was to have no treats. I hesitated in my reply, then retreated.

"You've just had lunch, honey," I told her.

"But I'm really hungry," she continued, with a hint of a whimper in her voice.

"You can't be hungry," I said. "You just had lunch."

"Uh huh. I'm still hungry."

I began to get annoyed, for she was standing between me and the football game I missed yesterday. I tried ignoring her, but it didn't work.

She stood there and whined, "Daddy, I want M&Ms."

At this point, I decided I would try to reason with her. I explained why she shouldn't have any more to eat. I used medical reasons, monetary ones, even spiritual arguments. My debating skills were superb, and the logic was overpowering. But my daughter didn't flinch an inch.

"Now can I have some M&Ms?" she asked after I finished my dialogue.

Then I got angry and attempted to extricate her from in front of the television. She still wouldn't budge and only whined louder. I next resorted to threats. This too failed. I contemplated all sorts of ways to distract her attention, offering to read every book on her shelf. I promised her rides and other fun things. She took all this in and concluded: "Daddy, can I have some M&Ms now?"

Any normal child would have seen the many reasons why she couldn't have candy at 1:15 in the afternoon. Any normal child would have been quelled at the threats. Any normal child would have given up trying.

And, as any father, I gave in and gave her the candy. My only command, as I handed over the loot, was that she not tell her mother. She dutifully promised silence.

But, of course, ten seconds after Kathy got home, my daughter spilled the beans and ruined the other half of my afternoon. I still don't know where I went wrong.

My daughter and I had a translation problem. We could hear every word the other person was saying, but we had not understood what was being communicated. Since communication consists of a shared understanding of concepts and not simply a knowledge of a shared vocabulary, we were literally speaking different dialects. Mine was rhetorical and autocratic. Its verbs were active and imperative, demanding a ready, listening ear. Her verbs were personal and oblique, totally mystifying the weak-willed father-figure.

Father-God knows how this translation problem operates. He once stated, " 'For my thoughts are not your thoughts, neither are your ways my ways,' declares the LORD" (Isaiah 55:8). Of course, I am not comparing my communication foibles with God's uniqueness. No matter how far regeneration changes us, our thoughts will never be what His thoughts are. But Father-God takes the responsibility for bridging the communication gap between Himself and His children. And the responsibility for bridging the communication gap between fathers and their children rests on fathers.

Some of the methods that God employed to translate truth to His children have been copied by most of us. But some of them have remained untouched. As with every chapter, the methods that have been chosen for examination are not exhaustive. God will never be finished in His variegated attempts to get His point across to humanity. However, the methods I have chosen to consider are the most common approaches God has utilized.

What They See Is What You're Saying

Suppose you had a son. And suppose he shirked all of his responsibilities and went out and did one of the worst things he could ever do to disobey you. Then, to top it off, he tried to make it look like someone else did it. When that didn't work, he tried to cover it up. This cover-up fooled few people (except your son who was now miserable, guilty and led to believe by his own twisted logic that he had committed the perfect crime). Yet he could not face you, even though he suspected that you knew all about what he had done.

Is there anything that can bridge the guilt gap and communicate both love and correction to this child? God found a way—with a son named David.

The story recounted above will live in infamy. It is the account of David's adultery with Bathsheba. It is about the murder of Uriah, the innocent husband. This is a triple bill of horrors when we consider that David left the matter alone for many months, even until after the child of the adulterous union had been born. Still he would not repent.

He had nothing to say to his Father. Wild horses could not drag him from his throne room to the meeting-place with God. And his throne room slowly became his spiritual tomb as he was locked in by his sense of having failed God.

In Second Samuel 12 we see Father-God quietly opening the lines of communication. We read:

> The LORD sent Nathan to David. When he came to him, he said, "There were two men in a certain town, one rich and the other poor. The rich man had a very large number of sheep and cattle, but the poor man had nothing except one little ewe lamb he had bought. He raised it, and it grew up with him and his children. It shared his food, drank from his cup and even slept in his arms. It was like a daughter to him.
>
> "Now a traveler came to the rich man, but the rich man refrained from taking one of his own sheep or cattle to prepare a meal for the traveler who had come to him. Instead, he took the ewe lamb that belonged to the poor man and prepared it for the one who had come to him." (12:1–4)

When God chooses a word picture, no one misses the point. Catch hold of the pathos here. The rich man owns many sheep and cattle. The poor man is not only poor, but he has only one lamb, and it is a pet. He and his family feed it and sleep with it. God even has Nathan the prophet call this little lamb a "she."

Above all this, it is David, the shepherd, to whom this picture comes. He no doubt remembered the ewe lambs he tenderly held as he beat off lions and bears.

As he listens to this tale, the blood that had come to run slow due to deception, lies and murder, now runs with a fervor: "David burned with anger against the man" (12:5).

"The man deserves to die," David proclaims. Probably standing, he becomes a picture of the fearless avenger of right that he had been before. He looked this way and that to see who the perpetrator of the crime might be. God's trap had been set—then it sprung shut.

"You are the man!" Nathan said. God has painted a picture worthy of the greatest bard, and the meaning catches David as he brings down the wrath of judgment upon himself. Hoisted upon his own lance, David cannot miss the meaning of this pointed story. When he realizes that his Father has caught him, he says, "I have sinned against the LORD" (12:13).

Painting a Panorama on the Canvas of Thought

The trouble with children is that they have inherited the capability of being blind, deaf and dumb when it suits their purposes. Like the proverbial three monkeys, they may not understand what we are showing, what we are saying or how we want them to respond.

A word picture is a form of communication that skips the fighting and the confusion when disciplining children. If a parent chooses wisely, the right word picture can send a well worded message to the far-flung reaches of the most closed minds. A word picture can paint a panorama on the canvas of thought. No matter how impenetrable a child is, he can always understand the meaning of a picture. Here are five things to remember when using a word picture to communicate with your children.

1. *Choose a subject that the child is familiar with*—God chose shepherding, a subject David knew a lot about.
2. *Touch the emotions with the picture*—God has the pet lamb slaughtered. Other emotions such as humor, anger, sadness and fear may also be employed.
3. *Use contributing details*—God added details that reinforced the overall picture. The rich man was very rich; the poor man very poor. The lamb was a pet and part of the family. But be careful not to throw in details that are irrelevant or distracting.
4. *Draw a parallel*—When you choose a story, make sure that it parallels the truth you want to teach. The more you have to stretch the parallel, the less effective the word picture will be.
5. *Give the interpretation*—Without Nathan's bony finger pointing at David and the pronouncement, "You are the man," David would have been searching every pot in the kingdom for ewe lamb hairs. The child must be shown the parallel.

Word pictures are not just for correction and discipline. They also can be useful for teaching spiritual truths. Indeed, the parable is the Father's chosen vessel for simplifying the wonders of the kingdom of heaven.

Over the past five years I have developed a rapport with my kids using a mythical bear family. Each of them has their bear counterpart, which I contort through a maze of images and interesting bedtime stories. Always in my mind is the spiritual mosaic that I'm weaving as they listen to the story. I can honestly say that they rarely grasp where I'm going—even though they know a moral comes at the end of each tale.

Once we spoke about the danger of white lies. Another time we spoke about respecting God and letting Him have the final say in our lives. Other yarns have been about healing, stealing and even male-female relationships. My kids do not tire of these stories (at least they've never told me so), and they have remembered some of the lessons years later.

However, word pictures are also effective when dealing with unpleasant situations. One of our children had a bad habit of putting herself down in front of other people. If the teacher would praise her, she would question the teacher's motives. If we built her up, she would tell us we were lying. This negative attitude was becoming a psychological epidemic. It finally came to the point where all she did was mope and whine.

Schoolwork suffered. Home life was harried. Her siblings became annoyed and refused to take the vitriolic malaise any longer. But no matter how many times my wife and I emphasized our love for her, it was disbelieved, pushed away and rebuffed.

Kathy and I decided we needed to employ a word picture. We sat the child down one afternoon when we knew we wouldn't be interrupted.

The premise we built the story on was simple. Our girl loved to give gifts to people. It was her favorite hobby. Anything lying around, old or new, was grist for the gift-giving mill. We used this as the central focus.

Here's the story: once, a young girl had some friends that she cared for dearly. As was her custom, she would make beautiful paintings to give to her friends. She loved each one and wanted them to know and receive her love.

One day the girl finally gave the gifts to her friends. They seemed happy to receive them, and they took them home. She was pleased that her gifts of love would hang in the homes of her beloved comrades. Then she set out to visit each of the three to find out how they liked the love gifts.

The first home had no one inside, so she peeked in the window. She looked around for her painting, but it was not to be found. As she rounded one corner of the house, she spotted it in a trash can, with a great big rip in it. It had obviously been dropped by accident and then discarded as not very important. That friend had no love gift.

At the second home she was welcomed in. When she asked about the painting, the friend said, "I gave it away." When the girl asked why, the friend said, "I don't believe that I am able to be loved. I gave it to another person I thought you liked better than me."

The girl went sorrowfully to the third house. Here, she was met at the door. "Here is your painting," the friend said. "I cannot believe you love me. No one loves me. I cannot stand to see this painting which mocks me with your taunting."

As our child sat there, tears came to her eyes. She knew that gifts were signs of love. We explained that we and others had been trying to give her love gifts. The love gifts were discarded, given away and disbelieved.

Within a few weeks we saw an impressive change in our daughter at home. She began to receive love and warmth. It took longer, but the school reports also began to show favorable signs.

Word pictures work because they traverse the canyons of words and strike at the heart of simple communication—a picture!

You Can Say That Again

Since the founding of the United States, legislators have enacted laws to curb deviant and objectionable behavior. Robert Wayne Pelton has collected some of these unusual ordinances together into a book titled *Loony Laws . . . That You Never Knew You Were Breaking*. One such law has to do with chickens in Quitman, Georgia. In this town chickens are not allowed to cross the road within city limits. I can imagine some city official swerving to miss poultry on the streets. Becoming angry about it, he enacted a law.

Another loony law is in place in New Orleans, Louisiana. It says that if a person bites someone with his natural teeth, the charge is assault. But if someone bites another person using false teeth, the charge goes up to aggravated assault. You have to assume that this happened more than once in New Orleans to bring such a stiff penalty.

In Hartford, Connecticut, children are forbidden to walk on their hands while crossing a street. One can only imagine that several dastardly felons disrupted traffic with this feat before the patrons of Hartford finally protected the innocent, foot-walking populace.

As laughable as these edicts are, most parents are not above enacting their own loony laws. Most of them are based on the fact that the average father is averse to repeating the same warning or instruction to the same child in the same way ad infinitum. For instance, in our house it is illegal to lock bedroom doors unless it is done to protect baby sister. It is equally unlawful to look at someone for too long (as in "He keeps looking at me"). The most heinous crime you can commit in our household relates to our car. Any child who asks more than ten times, "Are we there yet?" on a trip of less than fifty miles gets sold at the next stop!

Parents hate to repeat themselves. And children hate to have things repeated. So it would seem that repetition is out when it comes to good fatherly communication.

Wrong. Creative redundancy is a biblically approved and quite effective way to convey a valuable piece of information. God often repeated Himself in order to get the point across. Let's explore some examples.

How many times can one person say, "Be strong and courageous" in one lecture? According to God, at least four times. In Joshua, the Lord uses that same phrase repeatedly. Was God running out of material? Hardly! In fact, these four "Be strong and courageous" statements form the outline for what God was teaching Joshua.

God speaks the first one (1:6) as an encouragement for Joshua to be a strong leader. The second time God speaks it (1:7), He tells Joshua to be steadfast in obeying His law. The third mention (1:9) reminds Joshua of God's presence. The fourth time (1:18) the phrase is used, God reaffirms that even civil disobedience will not overcome Joshua. God uses the four repeated statements to build the goals for Joshua's leadership:

1. Be a man who leads;
2. Be a man of My law;
3. Be a man of worship and prayer;
4. Leave the rest to Me.

Consider also Psalm 136. Every line contains the phrase "His love endures forever." In our congregation we have had the men read the portion that modifies and the women read "His love endures forever." Since the first time we did this, the whole church remembers what is found in Psalm 136.

The name of the fifth book of Moses, Deuteronomy, literally means "The Second Law." God had Moses reiterate the teachings found in the first four books. Not only was this a different generation, this was also a people called to a different world. The old generation had been slaves in Egypt. This new generation was to enter the Promised Land. And beyond repeating the Law, He ordered that every subsequent generation teach the law *continuously* to the next generation (Deuteronomy 6:4–9).

It becomes clear as I study the repetition method of the Father that He uses creative ways to repeat the same thing. In order to show His covenant love for His people,

He inspires songs, He uses prophets, He pours out blessings and He lets His people know who gave them the blessings.

Nowhere is God more creatively redundant than in the book of Hosea. Beeri had a son, Hosea. We can only assume that he would have wanted the best for his boy: a good home, a nice wife, maybe a few obedient grandchildren. What Beeri didn't realize is that Father-God was calling the shots in young Hosea's life.

In chapter 1 we read this commandment given by God to Hosea: "Go, take to yourself an adulterous wife and children of unfaithfulness, because the land is guilty of the vilest adultery in departing from the LORD" (1:2). We're not sure if he married a woman who was morally "loose" or if he chose a woman that God showed him would be unfaithful.

Gomer, his wife, left him and prostituted herself to other men. We are told as we read the book that Gomer is a picture of Israel and Hosea is a picture of God. God expresses anger toward His "bride" because she has run after other gods even as Gomer chased after other men.

In order to paint a picture of His love, God has Hosea go to his unfaithful wife. By this time her prostitution has led her into a life of slavery. In Hosea 3:2 it says, "So I bought her for fifteen shekels of silver and about a homer and a lethek of barley. Then I told her, 'You are to live with me many days; you must not be a prostitute or be intimate with any man, and I will live with you.'"

God's message to Israel is poignant and repetitive: "I love you. I will forgive you. I will come to you and redeem you." The manifold ways and means that God employs indicate that it is necessary for us to keep repeating the important things our children must know while at the same time finding different avenues with which to explore the truths.

Where the other communication methods I mention center on God's forthright communication to His children, the idea of repetition shows that the methods should be put together in collective and creative combinations.

"Did You Clean Your Bedroom?"

Kathy and I have long felt that a child's bedroom is his personal castle—that explains the "moat" of dirt floating around it. It also explains why we need a drawbridge to get into it. Has there ever been a child who has repeatedly and effectively cleaned his bedroom without constant repetitive reminders and/or cajoling? If your house is like ours, a regular part of every daily routine is to ask, "Did you clean up your bedroom?" Like David Letterman, I have compiled a list of the Top Ten answers to this question, starting with the least frequent:

10. "Yes."
9. "John messed it up after I cleaned it" (to which the other brother responds and says that it happened the other way around; from this I glean that neither bedroom is clean).
8. "Do I have to?"
7. "Almost." (Ha!)
6. "It wasn't dirty." (Ha, Ha!)

5. "I'll clean it after school" (during the *one minute* I'm not fighting, watching television, eating my snack or doing the report that was due yesterday).
4. "I'm too tired" (unless I can play baseball instead).
3. "It will take too long" (even though they have claimed to have done it in thirty seconds several times).
2. "What will you give me if I clean it?" (no comment).
1. "No." (honesty is always the best policy)

I have often wondered why it takes so long for a child to understand that a clean, neat bedroom is healthier, more aesthetic, easier to get around in, easier to find things in and gets Mom and Dad off your back. But then I realize a few things about a child's bedroom. First, I never cleaned my bedroom, and I turned out semi-OK. Second, the child's bedroom is akin to our storage closet or garage. We clean those only when we have to and stick things into them when they don't belong anywhere else.

Nevertheless, I have decided that repetition will work on bedrooms. About once a month, we change tactics in the communication barrage we call "clean the bedroom." We have alternately reminded, bribed, helped, done it for them, rewarded, punished, inspected, shamed, praised, compared, lectured, used word pictures, made it a game, wrestled while helping, helped while wrestling, fooled around and kept charts—all curiously effective for a while. Lately, we have even reached the enviable position of having their bedrooms clean on fifty percent of all days (not to be confused with fifty percent of the time).

If an issue or truth is worth teaching, it is worth teaching again and again. Television advertisers know that if someone is going to buy their products, that person has to be exposed over and over again to the commodity. The school system works the same way: repeat, repeat, repeat. But just in case you think this idea is based on the three networks and the three R's, recall how many times Jesus told His disciples He was going to die and be raised from the dead. Even though they never listened, it did have a marvelous impact when He actually died and rose again.

It Takes Action

The Civil War is a gold mine of colorful characters and useful illustrations. One such incident points out the value of visual communication.

Colonel John T. Wilder, in charge of the Union forces, was presented with the latest and most deadly rifle, the repeater. It had never been used in combat, but its repetitive skills promised a quick victory. But Wilder had his doubts. In peacetime he had been an engineer, not a fighting man. He did not have a head for strategy, only for procedures. He was frantic as he thought about the following day's battle.

Early the next morning, he and two of his adjutants set out in a skiff and crossed the river waving a white flag. Immediately, they were brought to the Confederate leader, General Braxton Bragg. Wilder was a man of integrity, so he told his enemy about the repeater rifle. "Do you think we stand a chance?" he asked.

Bragg was also an honest man. Without a word he ushered Wilder out to the assembled Confederate troops. There they were, at least five times as many bodies as the Union side could boast. Then Bragg showed eighteen of the massive cannons that were poised to fire on his brigades.

Colonel John Wilder surrendered on the spot. Bragg had not spoken a word, but his actions spoke loudly enough.

We have all heard the phrase: "Actions speak louder than words." Never is that more poignantly illustrated than when the actions of Father-God are examined and displayed for all to see.

God's first message to mankind, according to Romans 1:20, was His creation. It categorically displays the "eternal nature and divine power" of our Father. In the words of a modern poet, "God was strutting His stuff." So the first thing God communicates to every man and woman is transmitted without a single syllable being spoken. As we look at the Rocky Mountains, the rocks themselves cry out, "God put this together." From the unseen mystery of gravity to the glory of the sun's perfect rays, God shouts in silence as His trademark actions breathe forth His holy and majestic name.

But God's actions get much more specific and profound than creation. One of these pinnacles of God's lofty truth is spoken in Mark 9:2–6:

> After six days Jesus took Peter, James and John with him and led them up a high mountain, where they were all alone. There he was trans-

figured before them. His clothes became dazzling white, whiter than anyone in the world could bleach them. And there appeared before them Elijah and Moses, who were talking with Jesus.

Peter said to Jesus, "Rabbi, it is good for us to be here. Let us put up three shelters—one for you, one for Moses and one for Elijah." (He did not know what to say, they were so frightened.)

The original language leaves little doubt as to what occurred. This was a step beyond glorification of Jesus the man. God didn't just cause Jesus to shine; He opened Jesus up so that His preincarnate glory was seeping through the molecules of His human existence. As Kenneth Wuest remarks in his commentary on Mark, "His Godly essence shone through the clay of his earthly body. For a moment, even the barest of moments (for we must remember these were frail, mortal men), Jesus was seen for who He really is: Lord God Almighty!"

So no one would be mistaken about what he meant, Mark used a Greek word to describe the change, *metamorphoo*. It means "to give outer expression to one's inward character." Jesus didn't step behind a rock and come out wearing a white suit that would have been the envy of television evangelists everywhere. Mark states that no one on earth could bleach anything that white! Without a word, He stood before them with the glory streaming from Him as water would burst forth from a busted hydrant. It is no wonder that these men were described as being in "the greatest of fears" (9:6, my translation).

146

Except for Moses on the mountain, Isaiah in the prophet's chamber, Daniel in his heavenly vision and John on Patmos, few others have witnessed such a spectacle. We have to ask ourselves this question then: Why did God invest such voltage in these men? What was He trying to say through the "sneak preview" of His Son?

Six days before, Jesus had revealed something to His disciples that caught them off guard. Because Peter had confessed that Jesus was the Messiah, the time was right for further revelation to be given. Jesus unveiled the final objective of His coming: not to usher in political change, but to die on a cross and rise again in order to bring spiritual liberation.

Peter could not fathom this, so he rebuked Jesus. Imagine, confessing that Jesus is the Messiah at one moment and, the next, repudiating His words! Only Satan could inspire such a flip-flop.

On the mountain, God the Father revealed Jesus to His children as the Glorious One. All the words in Jesus' vocabulary had not convinced Peter that He was bound for death. An action was needed to reinforce the words. Once the action was complete, God sent them back to the words of Jesus. The Father's spoken command to the disciples was this: "This is my Son, whom I love. Listen to him!" (9:7).

The actions reinforced the words and then called for the watchers to be listeners again.

Satisfied PKs

Dads may be fond of lecturing their children, but children must be shown how the lecture is lived before they

147

will believe it. I am presently working on an article about pastors' kids (PKs). In congregations I have pastored, there have been several adult PKs—most of whom were struggling with some form of bitterness for having a father who was a pastor.

My children are not near the age when they will leave home, so I sought the aid and guidance of several pastors whose kids were long gone. I chose these gentlemen because I knew most of their sons and daughters. What struck me about their children is that they seemed generally satisfied and happy about having grown up in a pastor's home. These were not victims, but satisfied customers of the parsonage. What had these successful dads done that others had not? I wrote each, asking them to respond to this question: what did you do to guard your children from events that would contribute to a bitter spirit?

The letters I received back captivated my attention. They were filled with pithy advice and straightforward, man-to-man talk. One man's answer, in particular, emphasized the need for the "show" part of fatherly "show-and-tell." This dad answered from his perspective, and he then asked his children to answer my question. One son replied this way, "Dad, even when I wasn't following the Lord, I knew you and Mom were not hypocrites. When other PKs said that about their parents, I could always say it wasn't true about mine."

Wow! What a testimony of God's grace! I could tell that this answer made an impact on the dad, for he wrote in parentheses below this quote: "Mike, you can't imagine what that statement means to me."

I think I can ascertain what it means—it means that it took a long time for Dad's verbal guidance to sink in. But the lived-out examples never got in the way of the teachings. This man and his wife lived out the character they were trying to communicate to their children. Notice that it was not an antidote for unbelief and spiritual failure. In fact, *there is no vaccination against rebellion and dissonant behavior.* This chapter is about communication, not guaranteed success. That's fiction; this is reality.

Reality says that even if you communicate truth impeccably, some offspring will do the opposite. But if your actions reinforce your words, then when the child screams out for an alternative lifestyle, he won't reject a second look at yours.

Hard to Love

Father-God is hard to love. His demands upon us are impossible. When weighed in His balance, we are always found wanting. God is perfect and relentless, a frightening and disheartening combination. I cannot love God because I ought to. You can tell me for five Sundays in a row that I ought to love God, but the fact remains that my obligation to love is hindered by my inability to measure up to His standards.

God can tell me He loves me, but so what? There are times I feel nothing from God—no presence, no peace of mind, no assurance of eternal security. All I feel is guilt. No words can arrest that emotion.

God knows how hard it is to love Him, but He helps us. He *showed* us His love. In First John 4:9 we read, "This is how God showed his love among us: He sent his one

149

and only Son into the world that we might live through him." Romans 5:8 puts it a little differently: "But God demonstrates his own love for us in this: While we were still sinners, Christ died for us." The word "demonstrates" literally means to "set up as an example of something." It's a present tense verb in Greek, which means that it is a continuous activity of God.

Father-God models love, mercy, compassion, integrity, faithfulness, forgiveness, joy, sorrow, power and meekness. For all of these, there are numerous living examples from the Bible. God speaks in propositional truth, spoken through direct communication in various ways. But His actions never nullify a single word He has spoken. Indeed, each act of God reinforces the words and invites the hearer who turned away to come back and hear again.

What to Say When They Say It Right

My sons were three and five years old. They were building some elaborate structure with their Lego blocks in their room while I tried to read in the next room. It was a quiet, rainy Saturday afternoon, and my wife was out. I was left alone with the waifs, and apart from periodic bursts of squabbling, the afternoon had gone smoothly.

I finished my novel and in a moment of satisfaction sat back to eavesdrop on the conversation going on between the would-be engineers in the next room. To my shock *and* delight, they were carrying on the preschool equivalent of a theological discussion. My older son was telling his younger brother how things worked in the world.

"God makes trees and plants them where He wants them. Sometimes people do, but mostly God does," he said.

"But what does He make them out of?" his brother asked.

"Old tree stuff lying around."

"How about rocks?"

"Old rock stuff, I guess," the older brother countered.

"Who gets to tell people what to do?"

"Only God gets to tell people what to do. And they all have to listen!" When I heard that, it sounded like a great summation of childlike obedience to God. I was proud of my son and his granite stand for God. I stood up to go tell him that I was impressed by his proper conclusion. But before I would get there, he added this to the conversation: "And I'm god!"

So much for good theology. What I was hearing, though, was a cassette recording of some of the things I had told them over the years, mixed in with some ideas that just popped into their heads. God had not showed them this; like any children they were playing mix and match with the truth. It is funny when children do it. But it is tragic when adults decide to play God. For the truth to come forth without sticky, cultlike appendages hanging off of it, there must be a planned system of reinforcement when our children finally grasp what we are communicating.

In other words, it is crucial that fathers learn what to say and do when their children say and do the right things.

Consider an Old Testament lesson from young Solomon's life. The greatest desire of his heart was to become a man of God like his father, David. In fact, David had impressed upon Solomon the importance of this by saying,

> So be strong, show yourself a man, and observe what the LORD your God requires: Walk in his ways, and keep his decrees and commands, his laws and requirements, as written in the Law of Moses, so that you may prosper in all you do and wherever you go, and that the LORD may keep his promise to me: "If your descendants watch how they live, and if they walk faithfully before me with all their heart and soul, you will never fail to have a man on the throne of Israel." (1 Kings 2:2–4)

Though Solomon was still young, he carried two massive burdens on his shoulders: the burden of the kingdom and the burden to follow God as his father David did. Perhaps these twin weights helped propel Solomon to Gibeon. First Kings 3:4 tells us that "The king went to Gibeon to offer sacrifices, for that was the most important high place, and Solomon offered a thousand burnt offerings on that altar." No one had forced Solomon to do this—and certainly there was no commandment laid upon a new king regarding the vast slaughter of livestock. Something was gnawing at his soul, prompting him to show his devotion in such a demonstrative way.

The omniscient Father approached Solomon that night in a dream and became the wish-granting Sovereign in a way all of us might yearn for: "Ask for whatever you want me to give you" (3:5). Had this offer come at a later time in Solomon's life, he may have asked for harems or riches or who knows what—but not this night.

"Give your servant a discerning heart to govern your people and to distinguish between right and wrong" (3:9). Here we see what gnawed at Solomon: he was scared to death of the massive responsibility of leading the nation. The burnt offering was the only means that Solomon could employ to let God know of the tenacious battle in his soul. In the heat of a heart willing to be consecrated to God, all other cares were burned away.

All he really wanted was wisdom.

"The Lord was pleased that Solomon had asked for this" (3:10). God knew that the young king's heart was seeking the heart of God. He had followed his father's advice and was now seeking to be God's man. Since this was a voluntary act, it brought pleasure to Father-God. As a result, He gave Solomon gifts of unbelievable value: lands, riches, fame and power. These were not so much a reward as a reinforcement of the righteous path Solomon had begun to walk in.

Whether it is an angry shout or a stern look, most fathers have developed a myriad of methods for communicating displeasure. This is not wrong—unless a father forgets to show pleasure when he is pleased with his child's actions. The Scriptures remind us over and over again that God is "slow to anger, abounding in love" (Exodus 34:6). He would much rather reinforce the good than punish the evil.

What does God count as good? Again, we can look to the example of Solomon's life: a desire to do things the proper way; a heart that does not look for rewards; and an effort to accomplish the proper thing without being pressured or forced into it. No one told Solomon the answer that would please God; his heart was so fully embracing the task before him that only a selfless request would meet the need of the hour. These three things (proper desire, selfless attitude, voluntary action) ought to be praised and reinforced.

God utilized many ways of showing His good pleasure to His children. Many times He rewarded them. Sometimes He audibly stated His pleasure. At other times, He gave His servants greater ministry opportunities. But in all cases, He let His people know that He appreciated what was happening.

An Ice Cream Reward

My son's Sunday school teacher was in tears one Sunday as I met her in the hallway before the morning service.

"I have to tell you what your son did," she started. I was not looking forward to this, but I was about to get a big jolt.

"We were talking about divine healing today. John told us how he had arthritis when he was a baby. He also told us that God used the arthritis to show His will to you and Kathy. Then he went on to share how God eventually healed his knee. When he finished, several of the other children shared their testimonies of healing as well."

When I heard this, I too began to cry. I brushed the tears aside as I prepared to enter the sanctuary. But even as I tried to concentrate on the service, I could only think of what my son had shared, and how he had taken all we had told him and shared it in a selfless, loving way.

When we got home, I made up my mind to show my pleasure to him. After lunch, I asked if he wanted to go for a drive with me. We went down to the ice cream store, and I let him order anything he wanted. Then I told him how pleased I was with him for sharing the healing story in his Sunday school class. After we were done with our ice cream, I decided to share more of the details concerning his healing that he didn't know.

He was fascinated by it all. The ebb and flow of our family life connected with his experience, and he felt more a part of a divine plan. Before we left, we prayed together. I felt a bond begin to form that has continued to this day.

It therefore was not a surprise when two weeks later, he gave his life over to Jesus in a full surrender of his will!

When the Times Get Tough

Contemplating Widowhood

taken from
By an Unfamiliar Path

by Arlene Peters

Why isn't Dave home yet? I wondered as the three of us waited impatiently. He had been gone a week and we missed him. Kurt was three years old and Karla only a few months old.

Well, I would bake a batch of cookies as a "welcome home" present. Dave usually came home from those trips craving sweets. This time I would be ready.

It was almost suppertime when my neighbor knocked on the door.

"Has Dave come home yet?" she asked.

When she heard that he had not, she added, "I don't want to alarm you, but I read in the newspaper today about a plane accident in Herrera last night."

Responding to my ignorance and surprise, she ran and got the paper. Sure enough, there had been an accident at the airport in Herrera, Columbia. Several passengers as well as the pilot had been killed and several others had been seriously injured. The time of the accident coincided with the time I assumed Dave would be leaving to come home.

I took consolation in the fact that the paper, while it didn't list the names of the victims, also did not state, "Gringo killed in plane crash." Surely if a foreigner had been killed out there in the Andean wilderness it would have been mentioned.

My neighbor offered to drive over to the nearest police post to see if they had any further word on the accident. Nothing. I could only adopt the attitude of wait and see.

Israel, the local pastor, was on the trip with Dave. His wife, Marta, came over to see what I knew. Marta was a fairly young Christian and I tried to calm her with assuring phrases and Scripture verses that I was having a hard time believing myself.

Eventually she seemed to relax enough for us to pray together and she returned home. We agreed to contact each other whenever we had news. In the meantime we needed to pray and trust the Lord to bring our men home.

Night crept slowly on. I tried to turn my growing fear over to the Lord but with the passing hours the possibility of Dave not returning became more real. When I finally did go to sleep for a short time I dreamed he was lying injured in a crevasse in the mountains where the searchers couldn't find him.

In the morning my neighbor was at the house bright and early with the newspaper. The only thing the paper reported was that the airport at Herrera would be closed until several recent accidents there could be investigated.

I spent the rest of the day pretending. I pretended that nothing was unusual when Kurt asked, "When is Daddy coming home?"

"Maybe today," I responded as optimistically as possible. "Let's pray that he does." Then I would leave him with his books and toys and go into the bathroom to cry, overwhelmed with fear. I was glad Kurt was young enough to accept the cheery words I had for him when I finally emerged again.

I pretended when Marta came over about noon. Panic was written on her face and it was obvious that she had been crying.

"Our husbands are in God's hands," I comforted her. "He will look after them." I hoped she wouldn't see my lack of confidence in what I was telling her. We prayed together again.

When she left I went back to the bathroom where I could close and lock the door so Kurt wouldn't see me crying.

This time when I came out I felt as if there really was little hope of things working out "right" in this situation. Dave was now two days late. No news was not good news to me.

Anytime now there will be a policeman at my door telling me that my husband has been killed. What will I do then? I found myself asking. Other similar thoughts kept racing through my mind.

Realizing that when the now seemingly inevitable news came I might not be capable of making rational decisions, I sat down with a piece of paper to list the things I had to do: contact Mission headquarters in Cali.

(I'd have to send a telegram. We had no phone.) Have them notify our families. Arrange to sell everything. (I felt I couldn't stay on the field with two small children and be of any use at that time.) And so the list went on, including how to dispose of our Pekinese puppy.

By this time my trips to the bathroom were characterized by anger more than grief. *Lord, how can You do this to me? You bring me down to this country and leave me alone with two little kids? It isn't fair!*

Night once again fell without news. By this time, I was sure I was a widow. I went to bed but I didn't sleep. I cried. I raged. I accused God of injustice. I grieved. I didn't want to spend the rest of my life without Dave. I tried to pray but my emotions kept taking control.

In the early hours of the morning I was in the rage stage. *How can You do this to me? I need Dave. The kids need a father. It's not right!*

Then, suddenly, in the middle of the struggle I heard God speak to me.

"He's mine, you know," He said quietly. "I can do with him as I please."

The room was suddenly filled with the strong, comforting presence of God. The rage and questioning gave way as an incredible peace flowed over me and I heard myself responding, "I know. Whatever You choose is all right with me."

That submission brought a serenity and trust I hadn't experienced for days. Maybe I was a widow. Maybe my children had lost their father. But we were not alone.

In the morning when Marta came over I was able to comfort and encourage her in a very different way. The Lord ministered to her too.

The incredible happiness of seeing Dave at the door later that day defied description. He was unshaven, dirty, haggard and gaunt from his trek and illness. But he was alive.

Later, as he told me his side of the story, we could see how God had ordered his steps and had literally done with him as He chose.

I told him of my meeting with God, an experience that became the foundation of peace and assurance whenever he traveled throughout the years of our missionary experience.

And whenever I was tempted to yield to fear I remembered the words of the Lord: "He's mine, you know."

Arlene Peters, along with her husband, David, began their missionary career among the Paez Indians in Colombia, South America. Eventually, God lead them to Brazil and then to Mexico.

Hope for Hurting Parents—When Grown Children Make Bad Choices

taken from the booklet
Hope for Hurting Parents

by Tom Allen

I had just finished lunch with the pastor. He asked if I had time to go for a drive into the picturesque mountains nearby. Sensing that he needed to talk about something, I immediately agreed. *I wonder what's on his mind?* I asked myself as we left the restaurant.

Two days before, I had Sunday dinner with this man and his lovely family. I remember thinking to myself that here was a man who had a wonderful relationship with his wife and two attractive teenage daughters. I assured myself that the pastor would not be sharing any "family problems." He appeared to have that part of his life well in order.

I cannot describe my complete sense of shock when this dear man of God began to unveil the crushing circumstances of the past month of his life. His oldest daughter had called home just before the end of her first semester at a Christian college. After a few minutes of general conversation, she delivered more stunning news than he could have ever imagined.

"I'm pregnant, Dad."

He was speechless.

As the pastor tried to continue with the story, he began to weep profusely. With my arm around his shoulders, I did my best to comfort him. Through his river of tears, he blurted out these words: "Tom—she's the apple of my eye—the apple of my eye!"

I was deeply moved by this experience. I thought of my own daughters—how much I loved them, how much I wanted the very best for them. For years, I have preached Proverbs 22:6: "Train a child in the way he should go, and when he is old he will not turn from it."

But in my mind, I was also having a reality check. I had heard so many similar stories from the parents I had counseled with through the years—good parents with "bad" children.

Dedicated to the Hurting Parent

It was at this same time that someone handed me a book by Margie M. Lewis entitled *The Hurting Parent*. [This book is no longer in print.] As I read those powerful pages, I was rebuked by the Lord for neglecting the wounded Christian parents—those precious moms and dads who did the right thing even as they had to watch their children go wrong. I was struck forcibly by the realization that some young people have had godly parents just like mine. But they made a deliberate choice to reject the love and training they received to pursue their own rebellious agenda.

This chapter is written to offer hope for hurting parents. Someone reading this may have just discovered that he has a prodigal child. Another may have been struggling for months or years with a wall of separation between her and her wayward child. These pages are for you.

A Warning

I offer this warning to any parent who might assume that he will never find himself in this category: "So, if you think you are standing firm, be careful that you don't fall!" (1 Corinthians 10:12).

None of us can say with certainty just exactly how our children will turn out over the long haul. God needs to protect us from the arrogant attitude that says, "My kids would never walk away from the Lord!" It is this very mentality which keeps many hurting parents in the closet. They fear that even a brokenhearted request for prayer may be turned against them by those who would judge their success or failure as Christian parents by their children's behavior.

Please read this carefully. I'm asking God to instill a new faith, confidence and determination within each hurting parent through these words. Those who have older children who are walking with God should express humble gratitude to the Lord for this immense blessing. And then they will need to gain a greater understanding of these truths in order to have a more fruitful ministry with those who struggle with wayward sons and daughters.

The Pain of a Ruined Relationship

It is difficult for many of us to imagine the agony of parents who face the reality of a ruined relationship with their son or daughter. It is a daily, nagging, haunting experience. At the end of the day, the question always seems to be the same: "What did I do wrong?"

The prophet Samuel suffered through the humiliating accusation of the elders when they pointed out that his sons, Joel and Abijah, were out of control and morally unfit to lead the nation (1 Samuel 8:1-5).

The father of the prodigal son no doubt agonized over the decision of the younger son to leave home (Luke 15:11-16). He must have faced many anxious nights wondering about the boy. Where did he go? What was he doing? Was he wasting his money or investing it wisely?

Have Motorcycle, Will Travel

I'll never forget the story of two parents in Kentucky. One evening, their nineteen-year-old son Mark did not come home for supper. He had left that afternoon on his motorcycle. In the middle of the first semester of his sophomore year in college, he just left. Several weeks passed by. No letter. No phone call. No contact whatsoever.

Finally, in mid-December, a clue arrived in the mail. A credit card statement indicated that Mark had made a gas purchase in the West Palm Beach area of Florida. The family had already planned to spend the holidays in southern Florida. Hope soared with the thought of perhaps finding Mark and being able to have Christmas together.

The parents received a tip from friends that their son had been seen working in a motel. They began to criss-cross West Palm Beach in an energetic attempt to find Mark. After several days of intense searching, they spotted his motorcycle. The father approached the front office to inquire about his son. He was directed to the back of the property. Mark's mom waited patiently in the car for a signal to join her husband.

After a few minutes of heated conversation, the father returned to the car to announce that Mark did not want his parents to find him. He just wanted them to leave—and leave him alone.

The mother wrote: "We drove away onto the northbound interstate, headed for home. Outside I cried. Inside I hurt like I never hurt before."

The Isolation of Shame

Many wounded parents talk about the isolation of the shame they feel. They are easily overwhelmed by emotions of embarrassment, inferiority, disgrace and incompetence. Egos flare up in the context of parental peer pressure to produce the "perfect" family.

Having been raised in what many would consider "the ideal home," it has taken me a long time to see and understand the pain of hurting parents. My first book was entitled *I Wish You Could Meet My Mom and Dad*. It was the story of how two parents raised ten children who grew up to love the Lord. Some years ago, however, I began to realize that my family life experience was unique.

Even our God, the Father-model for all moms and dads, has had trouble with His chosen children of Israel.

He has grieved over His wandering, rebellious offspring since the beginning of time.

Here is the question: if the perfect heavenly Father can be a hurting parent, who are we to judge the spirituality of ourselves or other parents solely by the behavior of a son or daughter?

Read that question one more time and allow it to sink in.

I do not discount the blessed truth of Proverbs 22:6. Rather, I feel that such a promise needs to be balanced with a higher law—the law of free choice.

God has not and will not violate the free will of our children. When they graduate from high school, they will be at liberty to choose their own course. The Lord is not operating a cosmic puppet show in which everyone dances on the end of His strings.

Sometimes the choices of a son or daughter may bring heartache to faithful, godly parents. But be reminded—it was that child's choice, not yours.

As dads and moms, we are responsible to train, develop and influence our children in every possible manner. We do this through our lifestyle, family devotions and family fun times. But it is entirely possible to execute these parental duties with real love only to watch that eighteen-year-old reject it all and go his or her own way.

This is the hurt that runs deep and wide. It's the pain of a ruined relationship.

We need to be resensitized to the reality of such wounds so that we can minister compassion and care for hurting parents.

The Problem with a Rejection Response

In the 1970s, newspapers across the country carried the remarkable story of a teenage boy named John. He was the driver of the getaway car for a gang of boys who burglarized a small business in a Midwestern town. But the story had two unusual twists.

First, the store that had been robbed belonged to John's father! Picture him sitting outside his own father's store while his codefendants are raiding and ransacking the place. It's quite bizarre. But the second aspect of the story was even more startling than the first.

Once the guilt of their son had been verified by the police, John's parents announced that their son had died! They even placed his obituary in the local newspaper. A funeral service was held for him which was attended by family and friends. From that day on, this wayward (but still living) son ceased to exist in the minds of his relatives. This was an extreme rejection response.

Karen's Secret

A young lady named Karen, nineteen years old, struggled with a dark secret for two years. Without her parents' knowledge, she had been through an abortion. Karen decided that it was time to tell her parents: "I knew that telling them was going to be the hardest thing I'd ever done. But I was sure they would be relieved to know it was over and I was willing to confess."

This is not at all what happened. Karen proceeds in painful detail to describe the trauma that followed. The parents were so overwhelmed that they didn't even try to comprehend her feelings. Karen's mother locked herself in her bedroom for two days. On the third day, they met in the hallway, and her mom exploded, calling Karen a whore. "I can't even stand to look at your face!" the mother exclaimed in dark, bitter tones.

Listen to Karen's predictable response: "I didn't think I deserved to be called a whore. But if that's what they thought, I'd be one! And from that moment, I hardened my heart, stiffened my neck and said, 'World, here I come!' I made a determined decision to take a plunge into the depths of sin and I didn't surface again for years."

This withholding of forgiveness from a wayward child and the refusal to accept or consider the needs of the prodigal is widely practiced by hurting parents. It can be a form of retaliation for the hurt and humiliation inflicted by that son or daughter's behaviors or decisions. Rejection can be the parental pathway to getting even—returning evil for evil because of the shame and disgrace that is so deeply felt by a mother and father.

It is folly to pretend that we cannot understand this harsh, unforgiving response from a mere human standpoint. But a twofold problem emerges:

First, the rejection response is self-perpetuating; second, the rejection response is unscriptural.

Rejection Is Self-Perpetuating

When parents fight back with either subtle or overt repudiation, it can be compared to throwing gasoline on a blazing fire. The scenario only becomes more volatile. Karen's story is a powerful case in point. Her response to being called a whore by her mother was simple: "Then I will become a whore!" Proverbs 15:1 states, "A gentle answer turns away wrath, but a harsh word stirs up anger."

We could be tempted to snap back with this comment: "But I have a right to be angry—my rebellious kid is ruining his life and ours!" However, in Christ we have the ultimate example of the resignation of personal rights. The sinless Savior who was unfamiliar with sin became sin for us. Jesus hung on a cross when He deserved to be heralded as a king.

Some Christian parents may feel that they deserve more from their children because of their faithfulness in spiritual leadership. And they may be technically right about that.

But we must be willing to resign that right. If we continue to demand behavior-on-command, the situation will only get worse.

Rejection Is Unscriptural

In Matthew 5:43-44, Jesus said, "You have heard that it was said, 'Love your neighbor and hate your enemy.' But I tell you: Love your enemies and pray for those who persecute you."

These verses present an overwhelming challenge. And we certainly don't like to consider this passage in a family context. But sometimes our very own children may become our "enemies" and "persecutors" through their wayward behavior. Especially then, Jesus tells us, we are to love them.

Perhaps this is the ultimate and most realistic test of the veracity of a parent's love. It is somewhat easy to have affection for children who usually obey and follow the Lord after high school. This could be compared to loving those who love you. But genuine love for sons and daughters is revealed in the tough times when rules are being broken and traditions challenged.

Christ offers another statement relevant to hurting parents in Matthew 6:14-15: "For if you forgive men when they sin against you, your heavenly Father will also forgive you. But if you do not forgive men their sins, your Father will not forgive your sins."

The forgiving person will be forgiven. It is as simple and profound as that.

Parents of prodigals need to refresh their own memories with regard to their own spiritual battles. God was always there for us through Christ offering forgiveness and restoration. Now we must allow this same Jesus to forgive through us. This is the scriptural response to rebellion.

The Principles for a Rebuilt Relationship

Thus far we have seen the pain of a ruined relationship and the problem with a rejection response. Now we must ask the crucial question: "How can relationships be rebuilt and love restored between parents and prodigals?" Three principles literally jump out of the father-son saga in Luke 15.

1. Unhesitating Acceptance

The prodigal son comes to his senses in the far country and makes a firm decision to return home. Notice what happens as he turns the corner onto the winding driveway which led to his house: "But while he was still a long way off, his father saw him and was filled with compassion for him" (Luke 15:20).

We should note that because the father saw the son first, he could have quickly decided against an accepting attitude. He could have easily chosen to reject this profligate boy who had pampered his passions and wasted his wealth. But miraculously, the father's acceptance of his wayward son was unhesitating. It was instantaneous and complete.

There is no way that the father could have known that his boy was returning in repentance and submission until he heard that heart-wrenching confession. For all he knew, his son was just stopping by for more money so he could return to his wild ways. But he didn't even wait to make sure that this young man was broken. The father's acceptance was immediate and irrevocable.

Bruce and Millie's Story

I remember reading about Bruce and Millie. Their daughter Andrea had married a fine young man named Ed, and they began their life together for the Lord. But after a move to Boston for Ed's graduate work, the simple faith of this young couple began to erode in the midst of the secular academic and social environment. They eventually drifted totally away from their commitment to Christ. With deep concern, Bruce and Millie watched Andrea and Ed cast aside many long-treasured values.

Andrea became involved in drama and invited her parents to attend one of her plays. Her parents drove eight hours to watch Andrea's performance only to be heartbroken by the lewdness of the risqué English drama. But throughout these months and years of Ed and Andrea's rebellion, Bruce and Millie kept their arms open with acceptance.

Eventually, Andrea and Ed's marriage began to unravel. One of Andrea's drama friends had attempted to rape her, and Ed no longer cared enough to help her through this emotional trauma. This daughter decided to move home with Bruce and Millie. Though they did not condone Andrea's rebellion, they also did not condemn her as a person. They accepted her, as Jesus would, even in her sinfulness.

One night, Andrea was seriously contemplating suicide. In the midst of her pain and confusion, she had a dramatic encounter with God. She later told her parents that it was like Christ came into the room and reentered her life.

Andrea and Ed were eventually reunited and today they are actively serving the Lord as lay people in their church. This is an illustration of the type of patient, unhesitating acceptance that is required to rebuild relationships.

Is one of your children waiting for you to accept him? Don't hesitate for another moment! Ask God to give you the spirit of acceptance. Just as we are accepted in our beloved Christ (Ephesians 1:6, KJV), our children need to be accepted by us. We need to receive our sons and daughters with the same grateful and accepting spirit with which we received them when they were first born (or adopted) into the family. Grown-up children may often behave in ways which will disappoint us. But they are still God's gift of life to us as parents.

2. Unconditional Love

Notice how the prodigal son in Luke 15 is not only accepted without hesitation—but he is also loved unconditionally: "He ran to his son, threw his arms around him and kissed him" (Luke 15:20).

We might have expected that this father would be waiting for the boy to come to him as he stood sternly with arms tightly crossed. We could even assume that he would immediately begin pelting the prodigal with rapid-fire questions: "Where have you been? How did you spend all that money so fast? You don't think you can just come home looking like that and everything will be the same as it used to be, do you?"

This is not at all what happened. In keeping with Romans 5:6, the father loved his son even though he was a sinner. A remarkable thing takes place here. The hug and the kiss transpired before this boy had a chance to confess his sin! And just as God uses the power of unconditional love to change our lives, parents must employ this same gracious attitude.

Joe and Carol's Story

Joe and Carol had waited long months for any word at all from their son, Tony. Holidays had come and gone with no contact whatsoever. Then late one night the phone rang. It was a collect call from their son who had staggered into a Holiday Inn about 150 miles away. Immediately, they were on their way.

When they arrived in the middle of the night, it became obvious that Tony was strung out on drugs . . .

again. His hair was dirt-caked and matted. His ragged, sweat-soaked clothes were covered with filth. The soles of both of Tony's shoes had huge holes from long days of hitchhiking. He couldn't even walk to the car on his own.

The father later said: "I've heard so many sermons about the prodigal son in a stinking pigpen. Now here I am holding my nose and living out that very scene. But what really hit me was how thankful the prodigal's father must have felt. And then I thought, *My son. I love him because he is my son. He has come back home, and that's all that matters now.*"

It took a month of gentle, loving care to nurse Tony back to health both emotionally and physically. And it is this active, unconditional love which rebuilds and restores the damaged relationship between hurting parents and wayward children. Do you have a son or daughter waiting to see a Christlike demonstration of unconditional love?

3. Unlimited Forgiveness

After the prodigal son had confessed his sin against heaven and home, the father displays his act of total forgiveness:

> Quick! Bring the best robe and put it on him. Put a ring on his finger and sandals on his feet. Bring the fattened calf and kill it. Let's have a feast and celebrate. For this son of mine was dead and is alive again; he was lost and is found. (Luke 15:22-24)

Parents often make the mistake of drawing up limitations for their level of forgiveness. For example, some would forgive a daughter for premarital sex if it did not include a pregnancy. But God's forgiveness is just like the father in the parable. It is complete and unlimited and available even before we ask for it. In the same way, mom and dad need to forgive from the heart even before that son or daughter would humbly seek restoration.

One father who understood real forgiveness made this comment after his son David had been arrested and arraigned on a felony charge:

> David told us he was guilty. We have no idea what will happen when he goes to trial. The publicity has already humiliated our whole family. But my wife and I have determined to show our love and forgiveness to David. We only pray that this will help him come to the Lord for forgiveness.

Thank the Lord for unlimited forgiveness in our Savior, Jesus Christ! And through His power and love, we can forgive in an unlimited manner as we rebuild broken family relationships.

The Promise of a Restoration Response

As we move in the direction of unhesitating acceptance, unconditional love and unlimited forgiveness, there are promises to be claimed. We can place our trust in the Lord Himself to bring back wandering, worldly hearts to Himself.

Through the years, I have been privileged to hear many stories that inspire hope for the most desperate situations. Some prayed for years regarding children caught up in drugs, divorce, homosexuality and other seemingly insurmountable situations.

But in each case, the parents had to carefully follow the biblical principles of acceptance, love and forgiveness.

These attitudes are liberating in this sense: As we practice acceptance, love and forgiveness, we are then free to release our children to God. We can commit them to Him for His safekeeping.

And the Lord is oblivious to time as we know it. The prodigal's father was characterized by his patience. He didn't try to chase after his son or try to drag him home. He didn't call him a fool or make him feel guilty. He just waited. He lived the kind of life, offered the kind of love and provided the kind of home that would eventually draw his son back to himself.

This touches me more than any other element of the story in Luke 15. When the prodigal son finally hit the wall and came to the end of himself, the first thing he thought of was home. *I've got to get back home. I had it so good there, but I just didn't realize it. I took so much for granted.*

May God grant that our homes will have about them that atmosphere which draws wayward youth back to both our families and God's family.

Hope for Every Parent

Finally, look carefully at these passages from God's Word—and take heart in His promises.

The LORD is close to the brokenhearted
and saves those who are crushed in spirit.
(Psalm 34:18)

Don't be impatient for the Lord to act! Keep
traveling steadily along his pathway and in due
season he will honor you with every blessing.
(Psalm 37:34, TLB)

You can be very sure . . . that God will rescue
the children of the godly. (Proverbs 11:21, TLB)

Tom Allen is one of ten children who grew up in a pastor's
family. An ordained evangelist, Tom has a national ministry to
churches and missionary kids' schools around the world. He is
the author of six books.

The Widow's Might

taken from
A Time for Mercy

by Marie Ens

I had first gone to Cambodia in 1961 as a young wife and mother of two small children. We were a family, secure in our love and companionship. Cambodia was a tranquil, tropical paradise. Now I would go alone as a widow to a country devastated by war and oppression. Yet the call I felt then was the same call I knew now. The strong arms of the Lord Jesus that had first carried us to that country together would assuredly carry me now—a widow alone.

Traveling from church to church to share the news of God's wonderful working in Cambodia, I pleaded for the support of other arms as well. In every church sat women who had also passed through the "valley of the shadow," saying good-bye to beloved husbands. They understood me as no one else could. Everywhere I went I asked if there were widows who would commit themselves in a special way to surround me and support me with their prayers.

One by one small slips of paper with carefully penned, sometimes wavering, addresses were gently passed to me by precious saints who had walked with God and knew how to reach Him in prayer. The list grew long as eighty widows pledged their commitment to form my prayer shield. I felt like their privileged delegate—one timid widow surrounded and supported by many Canadian widows, flying as their representative to help the thousands of pitiful widows in far-off Cambodia. My heart was responding to their sad plight. Musing on the calamity of their lives, I wrote the following words:

Sister of My Sorrow

Observe the Cambodian widow.
She is a survivor.
In some villages her kind
outnumber men six to one.
Once she was a much-loved little daughter, a
treasured sister, a chosen wife and then the
happy mother of precious children.
Today she is a lonely woman, plagued by
memories she can never erase:

*Fearful memories of a terrible tragic war
that tore from her side her father, her
brothers, her beloved husband and her
handsome young sons.*

*Tormenting memories of the day she learned that
her loved one had been wounded or killed and
would never again return to her.*

*Distressing memories of fleeing with her
little ones, endeavoring to seek safety
as the war raged ever closer.*

*Troubling memories of one happy day when the
war was declared over and of hope that peace
and security would surely follow, a hope that
was dashed as the sad realization dawned that
her suffering and pain were really just beginning.
A long dark blur of memories of endless hot
days toiling for the Khmer Rouge in rice
paddies and at dam sites in return for
a meager ration of rice gruel.*

*Agonizing memories of watching helplessly as her
little ones slipped silently into eternity, victims of
sickness and starvation.*

Yes, she is a survivor.
But for what purpose has she survived?
Of what value is her life to her now?
She languishes in poverty and loneliness.
That she has maintained her sanity
in the face of so much suffering is a wonder.
She cries out in her sorrow to gods
which can neither hear nor help her.
Her offerings of fruit and flowers and incense
sticks placed before idols of the Buddha
cannot bring her relief.

185

She fears the spirits and attempts to appease
them, but her efforts cannot bring her peace.
Lonely Cambodian widow,
I too have lost the one I loved the most.
Dear sister of my sorrow,
I have a message for you:

There is help for your loneliness and pain. There is
healing for your lacerated emotions. There is hope
for your future.

Your Creator has a special place in His great
heart for you! He has said that He is a Defender of
the widow. He has given orders to His people con-
cerning you, saying to them, "Do not exploit a
widow. If you do, she will cry out to me and I will
hear her."

Yes! There is a purpose for your survival.
It is this: You live so that you may know the
God who loves you so much that
He suffered and died so that you can come to
know Him. I long to share this message with
you so that together we may not just survive,
but live as He promised,
"A life abundant and free."

God responds to us when we are aware of our deep
need of Him. In my vulnerable state it was easy for me to
understand that I could not tackle this project without
Him. Over and over He assured me that He was giving
me courage. At a family picnic just before leaving Canada, young nieces and nephews sang a song that

seemed just for me, "Be bold! Be strong! For the Lord your God is with you." Without His gift of strength and boldness this widow could never have left the security of the arms of children and grandchildren to go alone to a country still wretched and politically unstable.

July 7, 1994

I was finally scheduled to fly from Bangkok, Thailand to Phnom Penh, Cambodia. That morning, in the quiet comfort of the guest house, I sat on my bed and opened my Bible, longing for a special word from the Lord. I was not disappointed. As I read Psalm 138, He gave me four wonderful promises (paraphrased): (l) He would make me bold and stouthearted (verse 3); (2) Though I would walk in the midst of trouble, He would preserve my life (verse 7); (3) He would fulfill His purpose for me (verse 8); (4) His love for me would endure forever (verse 8).

Fortified by His unfailing words and surrounded by the powerful prayers of my widow friends in Canada, I flew into my new adventures in Phnom Penh, Cambodia.

Parts of this chapter are adapted from an article published previously in Alliance Life. Used by permission.

Backyard War

taken from
Tears for the Smaller Dragon

by Jim and Jean Livingston

I t was 1968, Year of the Monkey. Four-year-old Mona
and toddler Tara were playing on the front porch of
our home in Saigon. I couldn't believe that the rau-
cous noise from millions of firecrackers welcoming in
Tet, the Vietnamese lunar new year, had not disturbed
the children's sleep. This morning, Steve, Kim Hoa,
Mona and Tara were fine; it was their mom and dad who
had headaches from lack of sleep.

Tet in Vietnam is like Christmas, New Years, birthdays
and the 4th of July all bound into one. It is a time to look
back to the past, to enjoy unhurried fellowship with loved
ones and friends. For a few days at least, *Tet* was to be a
delightful fragment of peace in this weary, war-torn land.

However, the tiredness Jim and I were experiencing
was a cumulative thing left over from the hectic Christmas and pre-*Tet* season. We had participated in dozens
of programs with Vietnamese military units. One especially exhausting day, a steady stream of Vietnamese officers had made their way to Jim's office with requests

for Viet kits or anything which could be used as gifts for the men in their units.

"Jean," Jim confided to me later, "this whole affair could be made quite simple by handing over all the barrels of vitamins and crates of relief goods to the officers who make the requests. But that would not accomplish our purpose or bring any good for Christ's name. Our work would be just another giveaway program, and that we do not want."

For these two missionaries, our constant pleasure was in doing something helpful in the kingdom of God. Thus, at this special holiday season and in the face of possible danger, our team participated in the distribution of some 30,000 gift packets in distant places. At each site Jim and one of our Tin Lanh chaplains were given the opportunity to preach before making the presentation of the kits and the Word of God.

Transportation to a distant military installation or lonely firebase was never a problem. Upon request, a Huey chopper or a C-130 Hercules was made available for our use, complete with pilot and crew. Tons of supplies were loaded in the giant airships. The team even flew to the large Con Son (Cong SHONG) Prison Island. Separated from mainland Vietnam by a distance of ninety kilometers out into the South China Sea were 4,000 military and political prisoners incarcerated for terrorist acts, murder, rape, theft and repeated brawls. Unknown to us, this 1968 pre-*Tet* visit would establish a beachhead for our Lord Jesus. During four later visits to these notorious tiger-cage prison islands, a strong church made up entirely of prisoners would be established.

Zoom! Pow! Pow! Zoom! As the New Year celebrations continued, the lingering smell of firecrackers wafted into our bedroom.

"Mona, come here, please. It's time to cut your bangs," I called. There was no response. *Why do children hate to have their hair cut?* I wondered to myself.

Suddenly a chopper zoomed unusually low overhead. My heart skipped a beat. In one split second I understood that the repeated, loud explosions we had been hearing outside our bedroom window were not the pow-pow of fireworks at all, but the blasts of automatic machine-gun fire not more than 100 yards away!

"Girls, into the house, both of you! Now!"

I burst into the study where Jim was working.

"Jim! That noise is not firecrackers. It's automatic fire! And it's down the street!"

"Let's go upstairs so we can see better!" Jim shouted.

Steve, who wanted to follow us, was told to stay inside the house and watch his sisters. We ran to the outside stairway of our building which led to the upstairs apartment of veteran missionaries Dick and Dorothy Taylor.

Two sleek Cobras, the army's newest and most deadly helicopters, were swooping low over our house, releasing their rockets and raining a hail of fire on a target nearby. A huge column of black smoke arose from the direction of an electric powerhouse as the rockets scored hits. With binoculars we watched American soldiers crouching on the porch of a house only seventy yards from ours, firing at VC somewhere below. Already bullets were whizzing past us and, from our position on the roof, we knew we were too exposed. We retreated to safer quarters.

Now what does a mother of four excited children do when a war is being fought in her neighborhood? Mop! I had planned to mop the floor, so mop I did. My heart was pounding, but I set out to do a very common task, one which the children had seen me do many times. I wanted to convey to them a message which even now is difficult to put on paper—like what not to do—like talk too much, like let your imagination run wild, like panic!

But the reality of our situation was beginning to clarify. We were literally witnessing a battle just 120 yards down the street from our house!

Tension mounted during the day. The air resounded with the crack of small arms including automatic AK47s. By now the communist troops were surrounded and desperate. American Armed Forces Radio broadcasted warnings every fifteen minutes. "All American civilians, remain in your billets. All major cities of South Vietnam are under siege!"

About 4 o'clock, a fire swept through the vicinity, burning several hundred homes a few blocks west of ours. Some VC were trapped, but many were hiding and using innocent civilians as human shields. One area near the Cong Hoa Hospital was hit and a row of prostitute houses commonly known as "100 Piaster Alley" was totally destroyed.

Our hearts ached. We watched scores of now homeless neighbors fleeing for their lives—a man with an old woman on his back; a mother with one hand balancing a bag hanging on her shoulder and the other tugging at a crying child; two Vietnamese soldiers supporting a limping comrade. They all came from the area just down the street from our house.

There was no letup of fire all day, and as evening approached, Jim laid out a plan. He took the family into the pantry-like room beside our kitchen where over a year ago we had dug a 5 X 2 X 6-foot deep bunker. The Vietnamese and U.S. governments had strongly encouraged this plan when the U.S. military began bombing around Haiphong and Hanoi. They figured the North Vietnamese might try to bomb Saigon.

The opening into the bunker was covered with an old wooden door. We never talked about that place—we just knew it was there if we ever needed it. Jim lifted the door and told me and the four children to climb down inside "just for practice." Over the past few months water had seeped through the dirt walls and had risen to about three inches deep. Several roaches and a dead lizard floated on top. The kids and I stepped down inside and Jim shut the lid. It was dank, dark and dismal inside that hole.

We practiced this routine a couple of times and then Jim addressed the children.

"If in the middle of the night Mom should wake you up and tell you to follow her, you must not say a word! Just obey. You will then climb down into this bunker. Do you understand? Remember, you must not talk. OK?"

That night a couple of neighbors worked out a strategy to guard the street on which we lived. Each man was supplied with a weapon by Americans also living on our block. The sight of this assault rifle both frightened and annoyed me for some reason. Yet both American and

Vietnamese forces had taken up strong positions on a street to the west of us and much of the firing was in the direction of our compound. What else could we do?

Our biggest fear was that the estimated eighty North Vietnamese communists who were surrounded at this time would break out in small numbers and force their way into private homes. Certainly they would kill any Americans. The western portion of our yard was protected only by a small three-foot fence.

All night long C-130 planes circled our part of the city and kicked out bright orange flares which facilitated night vision.

Lead zinged and whizzed across our house off and on all night. Looking into the darkness and in the direction of the bamboo tree just twelve feet from our bedroom window, I could see the red tracer bullets making streaks through the leaves. Several bullets hit the bedroom shutter.

It was close to midnight when Jim insisted that I get some sleep. Both of us were exhausted since the night before when we had been kept awake by the firecrackers. Finally I fell asleep, waking every few minutes to see if Jim was still on guard at the window. Thankfully the children slept soundly.

The next day the story was repeated, including the mopping scene. A heavy wooden window shutter was split open by a 30-caliber bullet that hit at head level a few feet from where Steve had been seated. Our house took at least nine hits—we had slugs to prove it!

Since early morning, after the first big explosion at the powerhouse, we had no electricity. The food in our refrigerator was thawing. I was forced to cook every-thing or else it would spoil. Then—how positively bi-zarre—the stove ran out of gas!

Jim and Dick Taylor decided to venture out onto the streets in search of someplace where they could pur-chase a tank of gas. Being *Tet* week, all stores had been closed before the fighting even began. The likelihood of finding gas was slim.

We had been told that the VC units had broken up into small groups, disguised themselves as civilians and were willing to kill for food. Therefore, before leaving, our husbands solemnly warned us under no condition to open the gate or allow anyone to enter. We agreed.

Jim and Dick had no sooner left when someone banged loudly on the metal gate downstairs. We peered over the wall from the vantage point of the upstairs porch and saw two uniformed soldiers.

"What should we do, Dottie?" I asked. "We promised not to open the gate. But how can we get them to leave?"

"I know," said Dottie. "Have you got any more of those toaster pastries from the World Vision ware-house? We will tell them that we have a special gift for them. Then we can just throw the pastry boxes over the gate. Maybe they will leave."

The plan seemed ludicrous, but it worked.

About an hour later, Jim and Dick returned with a tank of gas. Dottie and I related the story of our unex-pected visitors.

"You did what?" Jim all but screamed. "Do you know what we just heard? All the holiday leaves for both Army of the Republic of Vietnam (ARVN) and American military have been canceled. And there is a warning to have nothing to do with any Vietnamese soldiers who might be going about alone. The reason? Most probably they are fleeing VC disguised as ARVN soldiers! They kill and take the uniforms of the dead soldiers and then dress in them themselves. Good thing you did not let those two 'soldiers' in."

By the fifth day of the *Tet* offensive some 29,000 Vietnamese had been killed in cities all across the land. Finally Jim felt safe enough to drive the children and me across Saigon to the Alliance Guest Home. He returned to guard our house and property, his fifth night on duty.

That night at the Guest Home the sound of automatic fire caused me to venture out onto the upstairs porch. On the street below we watched as four VC were apprehended and, with hands behind their backs, were cuffed and led away.

The next morning the children and I came down to breakfast to find a number of our missionary friends standing around in obvious distress. Some were weeping. Our field chairman had just phoned saying that six of our missionaries had been killed and one captured in a murderous night attack on the Banmethuot Mission compound. Ed and Ruth Thompson, Robert Ziemer, Ruth Wilting, Carolyn Griswold and her father Leon had paid the ultimate sacrifice. Marie Ziemer was missing.

Alliance headquarters immediately ordered all women missionaries and children to leave Vietnam. Jim and I looked at one another in disbelief. Because we had only a few months left until furlough time, we felt at peace in requesting that we be allowed to return to the

States as a family rather than my taking the children to Bangkok. Permission was granted, and two weeks later we boarded a States-bound jet.

Home never looked so good! What a contrast were the quiet and peaceful evenings in St. Petersburg, Florida! The fragrance of orange blossoms floated through the window. During the wee hours of the night, I heard the singing of a Florida nightingale. Gone were the screams of Phantom jets, the clackety-thud of choppers, the drone of Hercules C-130s pushing flares in the midnight sky and the sound of exploding mortars in the distance.

At prayer time one evening I asked the children what they were most grateful for. Little Mona replied, "That there is no more shooting."

Yes, we were safe at home. But Mona had become an unexpected casualty of war. Several times each week for the next twelve months she would wake up in the middle of the night crying.

"Mommie, the VCs are coming. The VCs are coming!" Mona would wail. One night she asked, "Mommie, are the VCs over in Tampa? Will they be coming to get us?" I always snuggled her close to my heart and did my best to comfort her.

During the day, Mona showed no signs of disturbance, but at night the dreams recurred over and over again. Mona had experienced war.

The *Tet* offensive was one year behind us when Rev. Willis Brooks invited me to visit Tenth Avenue Alliance Church in Vancouver, British Columbia to be the speaker for his second week of missionary convention.

In two weeks I spoke twenty times. On Thursday evening the women of the church had a special program. After I had finished my presentation, Mrs. Brooks, a lady of very small stature, but a giant of a woman with a vibrant faith, pushed her little standing-box up behind the lectern where I had just finished speaking.

"Jean, before you are fifty women who know how to pray. Is there any personal request that you would like for us to remember in prayer?"

Immediately I thought of little Mona and her frequent nightmares.

"Oh, yes, Mrs. Brooks. I have a very personal request."

I told the women about Mona's nightmares of war, death and fears from the *Tet* offensive. The ladies promised to trust God and pray each day for Mona until she was delivered.

As I flew back to sunny Florida, I wondered how Mr. Mom had made out, cooking, washing and doing all the chores. I was sure this would be the last time Jim would volunteer like that again. And, of course, I wanted to tell him about my week in Vancouver.

That night I kissed the children and tucked them in bed. I had missed my mother jobs. I had missed hearing Steve tell about his seventh-grade adventures. Kim Hoa always had a funny tale about school. Tara was a happy little toddler who loved flowers and animals.

And Mona. As I went to bed there was one big question mark in my heart. I prepared myself for the usual. But Mona slept peacefully all night! From the day I returned from Vancouver to this very hour, Mona never again experienced a nightmare about war.

We could ask a question here. Jim and I had prayed for twelve months regarding Mona's recurring nightmares. Why did the loving heavenly Father not answer our prayers? We do not know why. But we do know that in His sovereignty, God sometimes chooses to use others in answer to our need. Perhaps He wants us to be aware of the value and potential of corporate prayer, the united, fervent prayers of His body. All we know is that God had heard the prayers of Mrs. Brooks and the "praying fifty." Our daughter was totally free from fear.

Today, Mona is a well-balanced mother of three happy children, a gentle nurse and the wife of a fine pastor.

God can be trusted in times of war as well as times of peace.

Jim and Jean Livingston spent more than thirty years ministering to the Vietnamese, first in Vietnam and then at the refugee camps in the Philippines. Jim and Jean literally sowed in tears and reaped in joy. Because of their efforts and those of others who unstintingly faced the dangers and deprivations of war, thousands of Vietnamese have come to know the true and living God.

Wonderful Complications

taken from
Near the Far Bamboo

by Martin St. Kilda

> *"Now it happens that this Candaules was in love with his own wife; and not only so, but thought her the fairest woman in the whole world. This fancy had strange consequences."*
>
> Herodotus

I was given a piece of sound advice: Always insure that pressures are kept to your outside shoulder and are not allowed to come between you and your spouse. In this way, as the pressure builds, instead of forcing the two of you apart, it acts to drive you closer together in loving reliance.

It's a lovely image that's aesthetically satisfying. But it leaves two simple questions unanswered:

a. What does it mean?
b. How is it to be implemented practically in a day-by-day, real-life situation?

Life in Asia was an atmosphere of unforeseen pressures in which we walked and breathed and worked for three years. How does one keep all of that to one's "outside shoulder"?

January 25

Mom and Dad Lewis cut the apron strings today much to my abject terror. We took a solo taxi ride to Prem Sadan Guest House—a lovely place: sunny garden with a little fish pond in which golden carp lounge in the afternoon. We have a very airy room that opens out onto this garden—the least depressing place to my tastes that we've stayed in yet. It will be a pity to leave it in less than a week and move in with our Dhurgastani family. This p.m. Joanne and I were finally alone after three weeks in Asia, finally a chance to find out how the other is coping. Walked to the Blue Star Hotel for dinner. Realized that I've been unfair to her. Scared myself, I resent having to feel responsible for her as well; also I have a tendency to accentuate her weaknesses and fears and thereby in some morbid, twisted way make myself appear to be adjusting better than I actually am. It is a diabolical, unnatural competition. None of this has been conscious (I hope), but I think it is how I've been operating. Must stop it, and instead cultivate a sense of humor and perspective. Might as well make the most of the situation and go through it all the best of friends. . . .

March 30

I've not been treating J. well at all. I give everyone else my reserves of courtesy and attention, leaving her

202

only surly tidbits. The guilt is worse because at present she needs me more than ever.

April 18

Spent the night alone at the Education Office's "escape room"—a place they've reserved for language students who are living in local homes, as somewhere to go when it all gets to be too much. A monthly day of solitude, silence and evaluation might be rejuvenating—but this one bore me no particular fruit. I could barely pray or even think, but managed to read a little of the Scriptures. Today the Symes had a little daughter—Mel and I went by to visit—a precious moment (that occurs by the billions). Joanne and I did get to have a good talk about us this evening—so perhaps the night away wasn't a waste. I pray we may improve—I must be more patient and sympathetic. Our worlds have drifted apart under the constant barrage until J. has no real idea of all that has been happening in my thoughts recently.

Is Counseling Needed?

When we returned to America three years later we were "debriefed" by our sending agency in Seattle. In our file was a letter from the personnel department in Dhurgastani that stated that, though we were wanted back after our furlough, it was felt that it would be good for us to undergo some marriage counseling.

We were shocked at this revelation, not because we had not survived some hard knocks as a couple, but because in our experience, all missionary marriages rub raw spots while overseas. The people in Seattle were embarrassed to have to make the recommendation; they were unaware of where or by whom it had originated.

Joanne and I racked our collective brains over the incident, trying to think of where such an ominous letter might have come from. We suggested various conversations, and then began to see a trend. Both of us could remember times at various fellowship groups where it was advocated that as a group we share more intimately in order that we might be of more immediate and vital support to one another. Joanne and I both took such invitations seriously and spoke of tensions that we faced around our household. Rather than the group continuing in a similar vein around the circle, each addressing the real, behind-closed-doors kind of issues and concerns, each time the group broke into heartfelt intercessory prayer on our behalf, and then everybody went home.

Reckoning that all marriages could do with some good advice, just how were we to approach a counselor? Hello. We're Joanne and Martin St. Kilda. Our problem? Well, while living in Dhurgastan under the most difficult conditions, we found that we experienced some difficult conditions. What advice do you have for us? You see, whenever we're under tension we feel tense.

Pregnancy on the Field

Because a pregnancy might hurry a recurrence of Joanne's Hodgkin's disease, the doctors warned us to not have children for at least five years. Plus, they added, do not expect ever to have children. The chemotherapy that she underwent had more than likely made her infertile. We are both the youngest children of small families and therefore completely ignorant of "things baby"; but not being confident that one wants children is a very different thing indeed from having some emotionally detached health professional announce that the decision had been taken out of your hands by the same awful treatments that had spared your wife's life.

God was very kind to us, and our first son was known as "the miracle baby" around the Mission. Living in Asia seems to cure ninety percent of fertility problems; and this accounts for one out of four humans being Chinese as well as for the 800 million Indians, not to even mention the population of Thailand, Vietnam, Myanmar, Malaysia. Mankind may inhabit the earth, but it lives in Asia. And it was now our turn to do our part; after eight long, quiet years our comfortable marriage woke up to find itself expecting.

Joanne was pregnant within two months of our arrival in Dhurgastan, and this kicked over a can of paint that colored all of her experiences during the time there. As strange new combinations of hormones surged and ebbed, as her petite anatomy performed aerobatics that we would have before considered impossible, she was unable (and forever shall remain unable) to decide which of her feelings were produced by Dhurgastan and which by her endocrine system.

We would awake in our tiny room up on the third floor, and our stirring beneath the covers would send the rats muttering back up the walls to where they slept through the day. The pungent odor of rice and curried vegetables being cooked over kerosene would waft their way up the rickety ladder from Bijou's kitchen. I rose hungry, but Joanne did not seem able to join in my enthusiasm over breakfast; and her appetite, never huge, faded away into a shadow of its former self. How must our hostess feel when Joanne's steaming plate was left untouched? And this became one of those times when Martin the hyper-missionary guarded the feelings of others at the expense of his wife's. "Make yourself eat," came my helpful exhortation, which might as well have been, "Here, bite into this live jellyfish!"

In Dhurgastan (we later learned), it is unthinkably crude to discuss one's pregnancy with anyone. This is based on several things: it might invite catastrophe from some unfriendly and meddling spirit; and, of course, the idea quite naturally brings with it thought upon immodest topics. Pregnancy, and those events leading to and following from it, are all quite natural and certainly take place frequently in Dhurgastani home life; but they are never to be discussed, not even between husband and wife. Why, it would be as if I were to refer to . . . but no, I can't even write about such things!

But we needed to explain the situation to Bijou who giggled at our confession (goodness, do these weird foreigners have no decency?); but as a mother of two, she understood. She told us that when she was "that way" that she had had to cover her nose and mouth with her sari as she stirred away over her cooking pots in the morning.

Pregnancy also had another odd effect upon Joanne, seeming to bump her gyroscope just a fraction out of alignment. Perhaps it was her changing center of gravity, maybe the want of appetizing food; but she lost her usual grace and became an uncoordinated klutz. In America, so slight a loss of coordination might go easily unnoticed, but in Dhurgastan it was a dangerous liability that manifested itself daily.

Bicycling over rainy, muddy streets through the maniacal traffic of Rajdhani is an exercise requiring the nerves, reflexes and finesse of an accomplished trapeze artist. And all this was asked of a pregnant woman pedaling uphill in a crowded city that does without any control of its sewage. The gutters along some of the streets we used are full of a black ooze that bubbles slowly; and you might recall that our route to the language school led us past the city dump, a place that after three days of heavy rain cannot be experienced by proxy. One has to do it oneself. Cresting the top of the never-ending hill brings no relief. It brings instead the wild, headlong rush of descent, dodging taxi doors that are suddenly flung open, weaving between unpredictable pedestrians, threading the needle through a dog fight that spills off the sidewalk and into one's lane.

Outside of the condensed muck of the city, out in the countryside things are not actually much better; one merely exchanges a certain kind of obstacle course for another. There are walls to be clambered over, walls that are lined with stinging nettle that is quick to reward a false step with a sensation like that of sticking a bobby pin into a wall socket. There are jiggly ladders to be negotiated up into dusty sleeping lofts. Walking along the dikes between rice paddies, Martin the hyper-missionary is trying to be cool because the village is watching, when behind him . . . splash! She's done it again.

October 31—All Hallow's Eve

9:15 p.m. Salyan House

And so my whole life is changing this evening. Joanne has just gone to bed aided by 10 mg of Valium, and Kerry White (an Australian nurse with the Mission) is on a mattress in the corner. Contractions are still mild, but they have definitely begun. The past months have gotten me excited about the prospect of having a family. I think back upon the few good ones that I have experienced as an outside observer: the Presslers, the Pardues, the Rabenhorsts. What do these all share in common? Each are Christian where Jesus is important to both father and mother, lots of love for the children is evident, other people also get included freely—there is lots of activity. And so now Joanne and I are beginning. It is very hard to believe. *Oh God, help us in this undertaking; help us to do it all as unto You—the wonderful as well as the painful. And Father of lights, aid and teach me to be a father like You: wise in his dealings. Responsible in his care. Firm in his discipline. Strong in his support. Diligent in his own ways and always in pointing toward You as the ultimate source of all good gifts.*

Today Joanne and I have two sons: one born in the primitive inconveniences of Rajdhani, the other in the modern inconveniences of Houston's Medical Center. The two very different experiences leave me strangely quiet—neither a frantic advocate of natural childbirth, La Leche League or Lamaze, nor a worshiper at the altar of invasive medical technology if its greatest motive is to prevent litigation over negligence. We have seen both ends of this particular spectrum and have found each to suffer their own peculiar absurdities.

Ethan St. Kilda was born on November 1 into a city too distracted to notice his advent, coming as it did on the last day of the meetings between the eight-member nations of the South Asian Association for Regional Cooperation. The streets of Rajdhani fluttered with the flags of Bangladesh, Bhutan, India, the Maldives, Nepal, Pakistan, Sri Lanka and Dhurgastan. The traffic policemen wore pressed uniforms and faultless posture. The streets were all but closed as scores of motorcycle outriders escorted endless heads of state and foreign ministers in their black limousines displaying their own fluttering flags over the front bumpers, all very high level and aggravating.

"You can't go that way. Outta the way!"

"But officer, my wife is having a baby!"

"Get on; that's an old one. Now beat it—the Grey Poupon of Rajneeshi is on his way!"

We managed to argue our way to the hospital, and my first sight as we hit the front door was a quaint one which we would not have had back home. An ancient Tibetan monk in his maroon and gold robes was on his way out; his long scraggly beard looked like Spanish moss growing from the chin of his wind-parched face. He placed both palms together and nodded reverentially, assuming that I must be a mission doctor. Inside, a second sight greeted us, this one not quite as quaint but just as unlikely—a dirty little girl, of about eleven

209

years old, with her filthy dress hiked up around her waist, was urinating under the stairs.

Dhurgastani culture and religion are very definite and do not shilly-shally with our Western confusion over the division between men's work and women's work. Having babies, to their old-fashioned way of thinking, falls very clearly to the latter, and Dhurgastani husbands are to have even less to do with it than Victorian ones used to. The wives like it that way; they do not want menfolks present either. Both sexes consider it a mortifying situation—just this side of shameful, and religiously it is definitely defiling.

I was not, therefore, as welcomed as I might have been at a modern Family Birthing Experience Center; the Dhurgastani staff only tolerated my presence because I was a missionary, and they could therefore not be sure but that I might be someone important in the hospital's budgeting process.

Joanne did it all without even an aspirin, not so much because of a theology which required birthpangs nor an aversion to epidurals; it had more to do with it being a harsh necessity. The last few moments were spent by me out in the hallway at the obstetrician's behest, and when that wee meow-like complaint first reached my ears something awesome happened.

Mount Palimar National Astronomical Observatory Internal Memorandum Colleagues. Please note that at 13:01 g.m.t. on 11/1/87 the earth was measured as having "reeled" upon its axis. Seeing, however, that no long-term or untoward effects of the inci-

dent have been as yet verified, and in the absence of any suitable scientific explanation of the phenomenon, this institution has officially chosen to ignore the occurrence. Please remember this in your dealings with personnel associated with the media.

The Director

In his biography of A.W. Tozer, James Snyder relates the story of the birth of a daughter after six sons. Tozer adored his new daughter, doted on her. But God began to convict him that he needed to give her up to Him. It was a struggle. Tozer relates:

> We dedicated her formally in the church service, but she was still mine. Then the day came when I had to die to my Becky, my little Rebecca. I had to give her up and turn her over to God to take if He wanted her at any time. . . . When I made that awful, terrible dedication, I didn't know but God would take her from me. But He didn't. . . . She was safer after I gave her up then she had ever been before. If I had clung to her I would have jeopardized her; but when I opened my hands and said with tears, "You can have her, God, the dearest thing I have," she became perfectly safe.[1]

I, too, came to the conclusion that God required such a decision on my part.

Endnote

1. James L. Snyder. *In Pursuit of God* (Camp Hill, PA: Christian Publications, 1991), pp. 187-188.

Martin St. Kilda is the pen name of Dr. Wade Bradshaw who, along and his wife Joanne, uprooted their family from the American Midwest to take on the challenge of a three-year-stint in "Dhurgastan" (so named to protect the Church there), one of the world's poorest countries.

212

Yong's Last Gift

taken from
A Time for Mercy

by Marie Ens

Yong loved the Lord Jesus. She had known of His loving care since she was a young child living at the Phnom Penh Alliance Guest Home where her parents were the domestic help. Happy and free as a little girl, she attended Sunday school at Bethany Church during the '60s. Then, as missiles crashed into the city during the frightening days of the war against the Khmer Rouge, it was the Lord Jesus Christ that her family cried out to, and it was He who protected them and gave them peace in their hearts.

When that war was lost and all the residents of Phnom Penh were herded en masse out of the city, it was the Lord Jesus who comforted and sheltered her family. She would never forget the message that boomed authoritatively from the loudspeakers of army trucks on that distressing day. Resounding throughout the city, the frightening announcement said, "Everyone must evacuate Phnom Penh immediately." Could it be true that everyone would have to walk out of the city? She remembered her family scrambling confusedly about trying to decide what to carry with them.

Etched on her memory forever would be the sight of thousands of frightened, bewildered people thronging the streets, slowly winding their way guarded by fierce-faced young soldiers, guns at the ready. Should any misguided individual dare to think he could disobey their orders, he was instantly shot as a warning to all to keep moving.

Finally Yong's weary journey came to an end. She and her sisters and their mother were ordered to join a commune with other anxious, exhausted women. Their lives were no longer their own. Every event of their days was strictly regulated. The littlest children were taken care of by the oldest women in the group. There was no school. Instead, all women and children as young as five were required to work. Daily they labored, cultivating the land, planting rice or building dams. At the end of the long, tiring day they were rewarded with a bowl of rice gruel. Those too sick to work were denied even this meager sustenance and soon died. Those who complained were executed.

Their beloved father was separated into another commune a long walk away. Cut off from him, knowing he was old and probably sick, Yong prayed earnestly for him. An idea was born in her loving heart. She would try to visit her dad. Even though she knew the harsh restrictions placed on travel, she would dare to ask for permission from authorities who had only contempt for those under their control.

Timidly she approached the commune chief and respectfully requested permission to walk to her father's commune. His chilling response raised frightening questions in her mind.

"Go," he consented, "but take your hoe with you." *Take my hoe!* Yong knew what the Khmer Rouge habitually used this heavy iron tool for. She had heard the horror stories of what happened to people who had committed even a minor offense against their authority. They had been forced to dig their own graves and then given a blow to the head with just such a tool. What would happen to her if she was seen shouldering her hoe, walking on a deserted road alone? Yet the compelling desire to see her father won out and she decided to make the journey.

Clad in the black cotton sarong and shirt issued by her captors, she hoisted her hoe to her shoulders and started down the silent, muddy road. The sun grew hot as she trudged along. Bright green rice fields dotted with sugar palms gave an illusion of peace and tranquility. Her soul found rest in the presence of her Lord Jesus.

By and by she came to a deep stream. No bridge spanned the rushing current, but someone had laid a plank upon which brave farmers could cross.

"O Lord!" she exclaimed in despair, "I can't possibly walk across this stream on one narrow plank like that!" She looked down again at the makeshift bridge. There, where she had just seen one plank, she now saw two! Calmly she inched her way across.

"If only there were some dead fish in this stream," she mused, "I could take them to my father and he could get some nourishment from them." But no, the stream held no such treat.

Hot and tired, Yong decided to take a bath in the cool water. Removing her shirt and tying her sarong under her armpits, she made her way gingerly down the muddy bank and stood waist deep in the refreshing stream. Bending over, she began to gather armfuls of the cool, fresh water throwing it over her head, relishing the invigorating feeling.

Suddenly, as she brought her arms out of the water, she was astounded to find not just water but a big fish caught in her arms! Her heart in her throat, she hugged the squirming bundle to herself and scrambled back to shore. She threw the fish on the grass and as it flailed about trying to get back into the water she desperately sought something with which to kill it. The hoe! Quickly she grabbed it and with one swift blow whacked the flailing fish into silence.

"Lord, now I understand!" her happy heart shouted. "You did not have me bring this hoe so they could kill me, but so that I could kill this fish!"

With great joy and excitement and a very special sense of God's presence, Yong continued on her journey. The sun was now hidden by dark clouds and she sped along, eager to share this delicious feast with her father. The fish was carefully concealed under her clothing since being caught with extra food might indeed condemn her to the blow of the dreaded hoe.

Her father's delight in seeing his daughter was immeasurable. As soon as they were alone, she withdrew the amazing fish from the folds of her clothing.

"Where did you get *that*!" her father demanded.

"Dad, you know me well enough to know I did not steal it," she countered as she told him of this wonderful gift from the Lord. Even as they rejoiced together they knew they still had a big problem to solve. How does one cook forbidden food so that the neighbors don't smell it, especially if it is a succulent fish?

The Lord was not about to abandon the project at this point. His thunder crashed and a great rain storm descended. As everyone scurried to their shelters, Yong and her father built a smoky fire. With the rain dampening the aroma, they smoked that whole fish and hid it away in his hut. For weeks he added small pieces of smoked fish to his meager ration of rice gruel and vegetables.

This was Yong's last gift to her father. She never saw him again. Still separated from his family, the Lord called him one day from the deprivation and oppression of that grim commune to the heavenly home he will one day share with his precious daughter Yong.

A Promise Kept

taken from
No Sacrifice too Great

by Ruth Presswood Hutchins

Fight the good fight of faith, lay hold on eternal life, whereunto thou art also called, and hast professed a good profession before many witnesses. (1 Timothy 6:12, KJV)

O n January 30, 1946, Ernie left very early in the morning for Tanjungselor. It was always an ordeal to say good-bye, but this time the parting seemed more difficult than ever. (Ernie and Ruth Presswood had recently been released from a Japanese prison camp in Borneo.)

"I will be back in five days," he promised. Ernie was a man of his word. I knew that if it were humanly possible, he would be back in five days as he said.

That afternoon I went for a walk with a woman named Satoni. She was the wife of John Willfinger's cook, Jahja, in Long Berang before John gave himself up to the Japanese during the war. Satoni was not a Christian and her behavior was questionable in a number of ways. She and I hadn't gotten very far from the guest house until I felt I had to go back.

"Are you sick?" Satoni asked.

"I'm all right," I replied. I felt weary. I just needed a good night's sleep on a comfortable camp cot with a warm blanket.

I tossed and turned all night with a high fever. The next day, Dr. Jasin, a Javanese doctor from the Netherlands Indies Civilian Administration hospital called on me. He ordered a nurse to stay with me in our nine-by-twelve-foot room which contained two camp cots, a small table and a chair.

I became so weak that I was no longer able to drink from a cup, so the Muslim nurse gave me a sterling silver, long-stemmed spoon to drink through. The spoon seemed out of place in those surroundings.

Speaking with difficulty, I requested the nurse to read from my Indonesian New Testament. She picked up the book and walked to the table where the coconut oil lamp was flickering. I waited and waited for her to read aloud, but all was silent except for the strange night sounds. No words came from her lips, though she appeared to be reading.

I tried again to make my wishes known.

"Please read anywhere in the book so that I can hear." The silence continued. Oh, how I longed to hear the Word of God for encouragement and strength!

Seemingly unable to get the nurse to read to me, my mind turned to the chorus " 'Tis So Sweet to Trust in Jesus":

Jesus, Jesus, how I trust Him,
   How I've proved Him o'er and o'er;
Jesus, Jesus, precious Jesus!
   Oh, for grace to trust Him more.

Did this Muslim nurse read in a way that her soul would be enlightened to know Jesus? I never knew, because in the morning I was moved to the military hospital and never saw her again.

The military hospital was a crude one-room Quonset hut about thirty by sixty feet which boasted only a dirt floor. There were two long rows of bamboo beds, all of them full. I was quarantined in the corner of the room by two reed walls and two bedsheet walls.

The doctor looked for symptoms of typhoid fever since it had been two weeks since we had upset in the Sesayap River. Typhoid was a possibility, but I insisted I would be all right in five days. I had had alarming fevers before.

My life seemed to be hanging in the balance. My mind went in and out of delirium. I had visions of an altar of burning hot coals falling through a grate down to ashes. I felt as if I would be leaving this world.

At one point, I turned my head toward the wall. As I did so, the Scripture from Second Kings 20 flashed through my mind. Hezekiah too had turned his face to the wall in desperation and cried out to the Lord. God had added fifteen years to Hezekiah's life. At that very time, when I too was crying out to the Lord, I believed He would add fifteen years to my life.

I heard everything that was taking place on the other side of my walls. Some things alarmed me. Someone had

221

given a patient an overdose of hypodermic medication. The patient lived, but only "by the skin of her teeth."

On the other side of my reed wall, a young Chinese boy had died. A carpenter was called in to make the coffin. The father and others of the family stood by while the coffin was sawed and hammered shut. The carpenter had a double challenge because the father kept throwing himself across the coffin, weeping and wailing for his son.

Several Indonesian girls took care of me with tenderness and love. I guessed that most of them had had very limited nurses' training, but when I was too weak to lift a finger, I appreciated all their ministrations.

Three of the nurses brought me gifts. The first gave me a well-worn blue handkerchief. The second gave me a well-worn pink handkerchief. Insignificant though these gifts now seem to be, it was almost unheard of to own a handkerchief during wartime in Borneo. Another girl gave me several things, something different every day—a bar of soap, a toothbrush and the like. One time she gave me a pair of pillow slips.

A day or so later, I heard someone being reprimanded for stealing. Pillow slips were specifically mentioned. Putting all the information together, I realized that the nurse must have stolen the things she gave me. She may have been dismissed then and there, because I never saw her again.

When I was on my feet again, I went to Dr. Jasin and told him about the gifts, especially the pillow slips. I wanted to return them. Dr. Jasin, however, refused to accept the articles and told me to keep them. It had been several years since I had used a pillow, to say nothing of a pillow slip.

Each day new people came into my life who were "friends indeed" because I was certainly in need. I believe my heavenly Father sent those people to help me.

Among them were three Christian workers who had attended the conference in Tanjungselor. I managed to gather together enough strength to ask whether Tuan Presswood was all right. They answered in typical Indonesian fashion *Ada baik—baik saja* (Is good, good only). They did say that he had been sick. The real truth was that they had come for me because Ernie was acutely ill. Seeing my own condition, they had decided not to tell me.

Finally, February 3rd arrived, the day when Ernie planned to return to Tarakan. I had looked forward to this day of promise, the day we would be together again and perhaps begin a life that could be called normal.

We could begin our marriage once more. We could be together in ministry. We could pursue the plans that we had begun to formulate from the time we first knew that God was placing us together to serve Him. Maybe we would even go back to Long Berang. These pleasant thoughts spurred me on to get better.

I kept praying that the Lord would give me strength. My fever had left in five days just as I had predicted, but what days of suffering they had been. Now I was gaining strength, but very slowly. I could even take a few steps.

I insisted on going back to our room at the guest house so as to be there when Ernie arrived. This was to be the first day of the rest of our lives and I wanted to be there to start it right! Dr. Jasin consented to let me return by ambulance only if I would promise to take complete rest.

I had no sooner got settled in my room when Mr. and Mrs. Van de Berg, the Dutch controller and his wife, came to see me. I thought it was a social call since they too had been interned at Kampili Camp.

But no. They bore the news that everyone already knew except me! Ernie had come back the day he said he would, but only his body. He had become acutely ill in Tanjungselor and had gone to be with the Lord two days earlier on February 1, 1946.

I could not believe it! I remember saying, "No, not my Ernie! Not my husband!" I felt faint and thought I would pass out. Mrs. Van de Berg held a glass of something to my lips, urging me, "Drink this; it will help you."

I took one sip and pushed it away.

"I don't need that," I said. It was some kind of alcoholic beverage.

Mrs. Van de Berg made another attempt to help. "We will pray for Ernie," she offered. That statement brought me to my senses.

"Oh no, you don't need to pray for Ernie," I responded. "He is all right. He is with Jesus. Pray for me!"

I later learned that Ernie had become sick with headache, chills and fever almost as soon as he had arrived at Bulongan. After the first day, he was too sick to carry on the ministry, but insisted that the conference go on. Sunday afternoon, the national teachers and deacons met in his room for communion. Ernie shook hands with them all and gave them advice and instructions.

Four days later, as his temperature soared even higher, Ernie began to be concerned about his condition. His attendants wanted to come for me, but Ernie said no, that I was not strong enough to endure the trip.

On February 1st, Ernie was able to eat a little and he was encouraged. He told the men the story about our upset in the rapids and asked Guru Tondok to pray for us. After a few minutes he said, "I do not want to talk anymore. I want to be quiet and see what is going to happen to me."

Later in the afternoon, Ernie once more called Guru Tondok to his side.

"Brother," he said, "I am very tired and cannot stand it any longer. By appearances, I must go up and that is far better. I just found out and now I understand. It is all right. Brother, I will go and enter a place that is good. Brother, don't forget your work! To backslide is bad! Yes, we must go ahead! Go ahead, and don't be afraid. Brother, I must go. The work is on your shoulders. I won't be able to go to Makassar, but there is nothing I can do about it. . . . All right, brother, I am so tired. Feel I must go. Tell my wife so that she will be all right. Brother, I want to go!"

About 5 p.m., Ernie took Guru Tondok's hand and said, "Thank you very much." His face was shining and his eyes were bright. He went to sleep again.

About 9 p.m. Ernie asked to be raised up and then to be put back down again. When the men saw that he was breathing his last, they joined in prayer and committed him into the Lord's hands. When they opened their eyes, he was gone.

The trip to Tarakan with Ernie's body had been extremely difficult and dangerous. Guru Tondok and several other men had started across the bay from Tanjungselor to Tarakan, a trip which usually took one and a half days. But the small motorboat had given out and they were forced to return and find new transportation.

Finally, the Sultan of Tanjungselor loaned the men his own motorboat. After the second try, they were able to reach Tarakan. Ernie had, even in the most difficult of circumstances, arrived home the day he said he would.

The funeral was held that very day, as Ernie had been dead for three days. Three days before burial in the tropics is a long time. They would not let me see him or attend the memorial service which was conducted by the Dutch officials.

He was honored with a twenty-one-gun salute. I heard the shots as I lay on my camp cot in the room we had shared. The customary native music and drums sounded far into the night to appease the evil spirits.

It was another seven days before I regained my strength. I spent the long hours on the camp cot searching the Scriptures, looking for promises in God's Word that would encourage me and increase my faith. But the promises I read seemed to be ones that Ernie and I had claimed together.

Then, from the depths of my soul, I found myself crying out: *Why was Ernie taken from me? I'm so alone in this place. Who can I trust or not trust? How much power do the evil spirits have over the people? Or for that matter, how much power do the evil spirits have over me?* Terrible darkness threatened to engulf my soul.

I didn't know what to do. There had always been other missionaries around. *What would Ernie do?* I wondered. Problems had to be solved and decisions had to be made. I felt forsaken, so alone. And what about our furlough, already one year overdue, which we were planning to take in May?

Finally, about two weeks later, a breakthrough came. I was reading Psalm 107:22: "And let them sacrifice the sacrifices of thanksgiving, and declare his works with rejoicing" (KJV). My sorrow, it seemed, must become a sacrifice of praise, a sacrifice of joy.

Although such a sacrifice seemed more than I could bear at that moment, a glimpse of light began to pierce the darkness. But a terrific battle still lay ahead, for it was one thing to read and to give consent to such a thing, but quite another thing to do it.

I realized that Ernie's will was not to be the ultimate word, but God's will. He was the One whom I served.

Long, lonely days followed, but the Lord once again impressed the familiar verses on my mind and heart: "I can do all things through Christ which strengtheneth me" (Philippians 4:13, KJV); and "That the trial of your faith, being much more precious than of gold that perisheth, though it be tried with fire, might be found unto praise and honour and glory at the appearing of Jesus Christ" (1 Peter 1:7, KJV).

Several weeks had passed since the body of John Willfinger had been exhumed and reburied in the European cemetery. Ernie had conducted the memorial service. Now Ernie had been laid to rest beside John. The real memorial to these two soldiers of the cross was the

Church of Jesus Christ established in the heart of East Borneo.

No previous experiences in my life shocked and devastated me like Ernie's death. Life took on a feeling of unreality. Surely at some point in time Ernie would return. Night after night I heard his footsteps coming down the hall. But slowly, I had to realize the awful truth that Ernie had come home for the last time. He had lived a whole lifetime in just thirty-eight years. He had come to the end of his Borneo trail.

We had been so happy to be together again out of the internment camps. Praise and prayer had been spontaneous. Now I couldn't pray no matter how hard I tried. Bewildered, I just existed from one day to the next. People were kind. They expressed sincere sympathy, but at the same time, they avoided me because they didn't know what to say or do.

The day after the funeral, Guru Tondok, who had cared for Ernie during his last days and who accompanied the body to Tarakan, came and offered to become a mediator between me and the outside world. I had very little money. I didn't know how to barter and trade, so Guru Tondok took care of that for me. He was kind and gentle and soft-spoken—truly an angel from the Lord in my time of perplexity and crisis.

One day, a young Dutchman with whom we had become acquainted appeared at my door. We exchanged greetings and then he said, "I brought back my wife. I want you to meet her."

"That would be nice," I replied.

"Where's your husband?" he asked.

My mouth opened. But no words came.

Finally I blurted out, "He died."

The expression on the man's face remains imprinted on my mind to this day. He was visibly stunned. But it was also a moment of revelation for me. Ernie was dead. It was time to turn my thoughts to my future. What did God want of me now?

I had come ready to serve Him, to lay down my life for Him if necessary. Although death could easily have happened at many points in the years just passed, God had preserved my life. What the future held, I did not know.

One thing I did know, however, was that my life was still in His hands. His will was my will. I was willing to live for Him and even die for Him. At times the latter would have been easier. But as Dr. Jaffray had said, "You will not find it so easy to die."

Ruth Presswood Hutchins and her husband, Ernie, were missionaries among the infamous headhunters of Borneo when World II began. They, along with other missionaries, suffered the dangers and deprivation of Japanese prison camps. After Ernie's death, Ruth remarried and has three stepchildren in addition to her own child.

Seasons of Life

Memories: Dealing with Reminders

taken from
Formerly a Wife

by Welby O'Brien

Sunday, the 12th

(Happy?) Mother's Day

Proverbs 3:5: "Trust in the LORD with all your heart and lean not on your own understanding."

I need to hold Your hand through this dark mess and follow *You* and trust *You*.

Saturday, the 8th

Went to the mall with Mom—I realized I'm *not* in pain constantly! Things remind me of Steve here and there, and that's hard. But I'm so much freer than before, like a big heavy cloud is lifted!

With the wounds of divorce still fresh, every year as Labor Day approaches I am reminded that September 2 was our wedding day. January 23 is Steve's birthday. Every February 14 everyone else celebrates being in love like we used to do. I hear songs on the radio or in stores that serenaded us as we fell in love. Yesterday a wedding invitation arrived in the mail.

Day after day, year after year, I'm stabbed with constant reminders of what once was and no longer is. Will each memory continue to stab me like a sharp knife blade, or will time bring healing and strength?

As I look to the Lord and continue to make healthy choices, I can anticipate with confidence that the wounds *will* heal though they may always be tender.

1. *As I force myself to sort through things loaded with memories, how do I release my feelings and how do I decide what to keep and what to burn?*

It makes me sad to hear of ex-wives who, in a fit of anger, destroy all pictures and other memorable items of their marriage and former spouse. For one thing, they can never be duplicated. There's no going back if for some reason they ever regret it.

But probably the most important reason to preserve photos and memorabilia is for the children. Regardless of the status of your relationship with their father, you and he will always be their parents. Pictures of the wedding and memories of happy days together will someday be invaluable and comforting to them. Should *they* choose to reject the memories, that will be their prerogative. *But they may never forgive you if you presume on their right to their heritage.*

I put away the pictures, framed certificates with our names, engraved items and other things that evoked strong memories. Emotionally, I knew I couldn't handle making any decisions at the time, and so I got the things out of sight to deal with later.

There have been times when I wanted to smash the fragile things to pieces, throw darts at his picture and much worse. One day shortly after he moved out, I threw a heart-shaped pin that said "I love Steve" at him and told him to give it to Susan.

Feelings of anger, pain and unfairness well up from my deepest parts as I see the sharp contrast of what was once my most beautiful dream come true having now become my worst nightmare.

The pictures and mementos of trips and other special times we had together trigger a cognitive dissonance that screams, "What's wrong with this picture? How can this be? What happened?"

Unfortunately, it's another necessary step in the grieving process, a dark valley that has no healthy shortcuts.

I gave myself permission to deal with each memorable item when I felt ready. Some have been much more difficult than others: my wedding ring, wedding pictures, pictures of us together, memorable T-shirts, an engraved clock, an engraved stained-glass hanging, books stamped with our names, gifts he'd given me, things in the house or outside that we worked on together, wedding gifts, my wedding dress, honeymoon and vacation souvenirs, and of course, the ultimate reminder—our son.

Some things caused me to weep as I simultaneously faced the memory and the decision of what to do with it. A few items I've been able to give away.

To be honest with you, there are also several things I still haven't faced. The wedding dress is still hanging in my mother's closet. The pictures I'll always keep because I know Danny will want them someday. I'm OK with those now, because I've gone back through them and grieved. I can move ahead.

And there's the stained-glass hanging with our names and wedding date. Several times I've almost smashed it on the ground, but couldn't. I don't know what I'll do with it or when. But when the time is right, I'll know. For now, it's put away in a closet.

Each person will have her own memorable items and her own best timeline for sorting through them. My words of encouragement are twofold:

- It's OK to cry or yell or feel whatever you are feeling. Remember to process the emotions in a constructive way.
- Take your time. Don't act out of spite. You can always give or throw things away at a later date, but you can never bring them back once they've been destroyed.

These memories represent a significant part of your life. Just because your ex-husband is no longer part of your life does not nullify what you had. We don't need to throw away the past just because it holds no future.

You are on your way to healing when you can embrace those memories as once very real, a part of who you are. At the same time you must release your expectation that to be valid they should have continued unbroken. The balance is that: you don't have to reject the memories because he is gone, but you must come to the point where you aren't dependent on the past. Pack them up as an extension of you, and begin to take your next step toward becoming the beautiful person God is forming.

2. *Will the pain of each holiday gradually go away, or can I do something to help?*

Yes and yes. Although each person and her circumstances will vary, as long as you apply the steps for survival, time will bring healing.[1] It will take more time for some than others. But there *is* hope. It *will* get better. In the meantime, in addition to processing your feelings, there are a few things you might consider as these inevitable holidays roll around.

First, be careful not to dwell on the past. As memories and their accompanying feelings crop up, let them come. Feel the ache and the sting and all that comes with them. When you feel a lull, take advantage of that crucial point to choose between staying there and soaking in the muck or taking a step ahead toward cleansing. As you give yourself a healthy outlet for those feelings, the pain won't totally disappear, but you will be moving in the right direction.

Another thought has been helpful to me, but because I'm not as creative as others, the progress has been slow. On the holidays that I must continue to observe (now without a husband), I try to establish new traditions. It has been helpful to talk with other wives and mothers to get ideas and also to brainstorm a little with Danny. The purpose here is to get the focus off of what no longer is and pave the way to building *new* memories.

For instance, instead of counting my Valentines (wow, one from my mother), Danny and I could make a card and

237

some cookies to take to a lonely person at the nearby nursing home. With joint custody, Danny splits the celebration of certain holidays between me and Steve. So we have had to come up with special ways to have Christmas and birthdays, even when they are not on the actual day. I've learned that's OK too.

Whatever I can do to refocus and begin to build new memories will, in time, help transform a day of painful reminders into a day of pleasant memories.

3. *Can I prepare myself in advance for the things that will catch me off guard and trigger negative emotions?*

One week after Steve moved out, he bought a new Jeep Cherokee. From then on, every time I saw a gray Jeep Cherokee I felt like puking. Sometimes I also felt like jamming my foot on the accelerator and smashing into it. Or speeding past and giving them a dirty look or choice words. All this from sweet little me.

Steve used to drive the city transit buses. It took me a couple of years to not react every time I saw one. In that case, it was probably the frequency that helped desensitize me eventually.

On several occasions I've been thrown off guard by music in the grocery store. I know the music is intended to put you in a good mood so you'll buy more. Well, they didn't count on emotionally exposed women recovering from divorce. The Christmas right after he left was the worst. I was at the supermarket in the detergent aisle. "I'll Be Home for Christmas" began playing. I was paralyzed as I leaned over my grocery cart, sobbing

He would not be home for Christmas. He would never again be home for Christmas.

I don't know if I can honestly say there's a surefire way to be prepared for these surprises. But I have learned a few things that have helped.

When possible, avoid places and things that trigger the pain. It would be masochistic for me to deliberately go where I knew I'd have to see his car or to a memorable location. I'm also taking a foolish risk by tuning in to the local mellow-music oldies radio station.

After doing what I can to avoid the memory triggers, it has also been helpful to maintain a survival checklist. Keeping those "tools" current allows me to draw on them at any time, especially when I'm caught off guard by circumstances.

The most crucial thing I can do as I progress from surviving to growing is to walk with the Lord. That involves a conscious awareness of who He is and the importance of a daily relationship with Him. Reading the Bible and praying are vital components of this walk. One of my barometers that indicates how well I'm doing is how long it takes me to turn to the Lord in a time of need. Just last night after receiving a very painful phone call, I stood dazed in the hallway. I battled the urge to turn on the TV and start munching. I remembered to feel the feelings. And then I prayed.

Ideally, I would like to turn instinctively to the Lord for help first whether I need to cry before Him, knowing He cares, or whether I need wisdom for a situation. I know He is always there, waiting for me, and I am learning to go to Him more quickly.

When my walk with the Lord is honest and growing, I can reach out to Him anytime. He is not caught off guard by anything. And He will help me through.

A sign on my refrigerator says, "Fear not tomorrow; God is already there."

4. When will I be able to tolerate sentimental music?

It took me a long time to be able to listen to romantic music and actually enjoy it. There were many times when I'd turn on the radio only to have my heart wrenched by some memorable love song. Sometimes I knew I needed to cry and this was the ideal catalyst. Other times I took control and quickly switched stations or turned it off.

As a music lover, this has been a difficult area for me. During the time when I wasn't yet ready to listen to my old favorites, there were a few things I was able to do which helped. My first remedy was to fill the void with good Christian music. I had not kept up with what was out there and was pleasantly surprised. Not only is the music pleasurable as I listen, but it's also uplifting. I come away a little stronger and with a renewed perspective. When I get my mind focused on Jesus, there is hope.

Another helpful strategy has been to expose myself to new music, whether Christian or secular. New songs and new styles of music can be enjoyable and culturally expanding.

Finally, a strategy which requires time: create new associations with the old favorites to replace the past memories. This may only work for some people, and it will take time, new experiences and maybe new people in order to establish the associations. For example when I used to hear Barry Manilow sing "Looks Like We Made It," I'd remember the summer before Steve and I were married when we were apart for eight weeks and thought we'd never survive. Now, I use this song at the end of my exercise tape to congratulate myself for making it through the workout.

5. What's the best way to survive going to a wedding?

The first wedding I had to attend after the divorce was a killer. At one point I was crying my heart out. At another point it was all I could do to keep from standing up and shouting, "Don't believe him! Run now while you still have a chance!"

As much as I tried to ignore my own past and celebrate with these newlyweds, I couldn't. I felt like a sitting target with memory missiles aimed directly at me. As each one struck me, I felt bursts of pain. Anger. Loneliness. Cynicism. Hatred. Loss. Grief. It was almost like attending a baby dedication after losing your own child.

I felt like the biggest hypocrite. What in the world was *I* doing here? Marriage was the last thing I had faith in. I had been where they were once, and look where it got me. Yet here I was all dressed up with an approving veneer smile, masking the remains of my half of a dead marriage.

In order to survive, I had to adhere to two key guidelines: Feel the feelings and make healthy choices.

About two years after the divorce, I attended another wedding. I looked great and felt great. Until the music started. My left brain dominated as I told myself, "I'm fine, I'm healed and I'm excited for my friends." That worked for about ten minutes, and then the right brain levy broke and the floods came. I realized I needed to let the feelings rise to the surface. I am not super-single-woman, and I may never be 100 percent over Steve. It's OK to hurt, and it's necessary to cry.

I received a wedding invitation last week. As a choice maker, I've learned that I can say no. If I feel it will stir up more pain and it is best not to go, then I decline.

Yet I am also free to choose to go, to choose to support and celebrate with my friends. It would not be good for me to nurse my bitterness by whining, "It's not fair. If I can't be happily married, nobody else can either." In essence, that's what my skepticism says.

There is a good chance that the other couple *will* be happy, and I choose to cheer them on. I also choose not to allow my disappointments and my marital corpse to spoil their hopes and dreams.

And just between us, deep down inside I have that same hope and dream to live happily ever after once again.

Endnote

1. Steps for Survival: 1) Saturate yourself with Scripture; 2) Pour out your heart to God; 3) Feel the pain; 4) Let yourself cry; 5) Talk to someone trustworthy; 6) Laugh, giggle, play; 7) Be open to wise input; 8) Write down your feelings; 9) Make sleep a priority; 10) Fill your body with healthy things; 11) Do some physical activity every day; 12) Be your best; 13) Treat yourself; 14) Let go; 15) Don't rush.

Welby O'Brien holds a teaching degree from Biola University and a master's degree in counseling. She is a conference speaker for ministry groups, divorce recovery and singles. She lives with her son in Portland, Oregon.

My Turn

taken from
Walk Around the World

by Rosalie Flickinger

January 15, Friday

Mother died today. Four days ago I was with her. Now I am alone, an ocean away. God, why did it have to be this way? We prayed for You to take her before I had to leave. Wasn't it her wish, too?

Was it only three days ago we boarded the plane for our next overseas term? Even the ice storm which caused us to miss our connecting flight in Chicago made me think You were delaying me. But You waited until it was too late. You waited until the cost was beyond what I can bear.

She really is gone. Memories. Memories. Memories. Mother, how I loved you! I counted the days we were home, a total of 159, many of them at your bedside. What a gift! But why couldn't it have been just four more, Lord?

She was eighty-nine and longed to be in heaven with Dad and with You. But Lord, this time the cost is too high; You've asked more than I am willing to give. I already gave up my new house and a lot of stuff. That was OK. I could handle that. But not this—not missing my mother's funeral. I need to say this final good-bye with my family. It isn't fair. Tonight I feel no comfort, no peace, no serenity, no sense of Your presence. I know You are here, but I don't feel it.

I received the fax at 4:30 p.m. telling of Mother's peaceful homegoing. The moment is forever etched in my mind. My mind was already in a whirl because of having a houseguest for the week. *God, I have enough problems*, I thought. Here we are house-sitting because our apartment was sold, and the house-sitting includes the care of the sixteen-year-old daughter of the house. We're back with no permanent place to live and not even the prospect of one. I can't even weep alone. I have to do it with strangers around, while trying to concentrate on preparing dinner for everyone. What was it we ate tonight anyway?

January 16, Saturday

The sun is shining. I slept well after having a good cleansing, healing "weep" last night. This morning I finished reading Madeleine L'Engle's *Two-Part Invention*. She tells of her marriage to Hugh—and his death. She often asked, "My God, my God, why have You forsaken me?" She says it is OK to ask why. Some of Mom's last words to me were, "I once read that we must never ask 'why.'" Same problem, two perspectives.

Madeleine, you've got a point; it is all right to ask why. But we can't do it forever. We must also accept what God gives us. That was definitely Mom's theology and so easy for her to accept. At one point in Hugh's illness, L'Engle wrote, "I am beyond anger, I am in a dark place where I simply exist in the pain of this moment. It's too much. It's not fair. It's statistically excessive."

I'm not sure what she meant by "statistically excessive," but I can't count the times I have said "it isn't fair" in the last twenty-four hours. I still don't understand the timing, but the bitterness is ebbing.

This afternoon we drove into the wooded hills. It was sunny and surprisingly warm for a January day. We walked deep into the forest to one of our favorite spots. I sat at an old rustic table, reading, thinking, remembering.

Mom always went outside to work in the garden whenever any of us children left after being home for a weekend or holiday. She said she couldn't stand to stay inside the house alone, so she went out to commune with nature. Today I know how she felt, except that I didn't leave her—she left me! What a shock! I had no idea how alone you feel when you realize your mother has left you. As usual, she was right; there is something therapeutic about God's nature when you are lonely.

January 17, Sunday

We went to our English-speaking church as I could not endure the thought of going to our German church where I would not be comforted in my own language. Earlier this morning I read in my *Joy and Strength* devotional book the Scripture reading in Ezekiel 14:23: "Ye shall know that I have not done without cause all that I have done, . . . saith the Lord GOD" (KJV).

The author writes:

Joy is the lesson set for some,
For others pain best teacher is;

245

We know not which for us shall come,
But both are Heaven's high ministries.

Lord, what is it You want me to learn?

January 18, Monday

Mom's funeral day. I could not go to work today. We
drove to the mountains. *Perhaps they can help bring some
comfort on this difficult day*, I thought. Dad's favorite psalm
came to mind: "I will lift up mine eyes unto the hills, from
whence cometh my help. My help cometh from the LORD"
(Psalm 121:1-2, KJV).

I'm still not completely at peace about not having
gone home for the funeral. I do hope I will get over this
resentment about having to miss this day of togetherness with the family. I feel left out. I'm not a part of the
natural bonding which takes place among siblings after
both parents die. Being with my family means so much
to me. Too much?

On our way home we stopped in Bern, thinking we
could meditate in the beautiful cathedral. It was locked.
As we walked away, the cathedral bells were tolling. It
was 5 o'clock, which meant it was 10 o'clock in Kansas
and time for the funeral procession. I thought, *What am I
doing walking the streets of Bern, Switzerland, while my
mother's funeral procession is in progress? It is like a bad
dream. I missed the train somewhere. I'm not where I'm supposed to be.*

Later, we stopped at a roadside restaurant for a bite
to eat. We couldn't even find a quiet gasthaus open. I
was eating goulash soup when it hit me: *I'm eating soup*

while my mother's funeral service is going on! Have I no re-spect? The soup stuck in my throat, tears welled up.

I can't even cry during my mother's funeral service without all these strangers watching and wondering what's wrong with this woman. I should at least be at home, but I have no home. Our suitcases are stacked in the corner of someone else's home. A teenager is there. It is her home; we are the intruders, and a houseguest is there for the week. *Lord, missing my own mother's funeral and not even having my own private place to grieve and weep is more than I can bear today.*

The family telephone call tonight reported a beautiful service. Many wonderful tributes paid, mother deserving them all. Too bad we didn't write them before she died. We need to give tributes to people before they die, when we can see the look on their faces in response to some kind words. Now it's done. She's buried. It's over. Maybe I can let go of it all and get on with life.

January 21, Thursday

Today when I prayed it hit me—I don't need to pray for Mom anymore! Made me weep all over again.

January 26, Tuesday

Read Job 38-42 this morning. God answers Job's questions. In plain words, God says, "Who are you to question what I do?" Job replies in chapter 42, "I know that you can do all things; no plan of yours can be thwarted. You asked, 'Who is this that obscures my counsel without knowledge?' Surely I spoke of things I did not understand, things too wonderful for me to know" (42:2-3).

Lord, I still don't understand the timing in this and very likely never will. But I know You are sovereign. You see the entire framework of my life. Right now I am only seeing a very tiny part of it and that part is crying out that You asked too much! Someday I may understand the "things too wonderful for me to know." For now, I can only agree with the psalmist: You can do whatever pleases You! "Our God is in heaven; he does whatever pleases him" (Psalm 115:3).

It has been several months since I wrote these journal entries. My hope is that what is most personal to me will be most useful to you. Henry Nouwen, writing in the preface of *With Open Hands*, said, "But aren't my own experiences so personal that they might just as well remain hidden? Or could it be that what is most personal for me, what rings in the depths of my own being, also has meaning for others? Ultimately, I believe that what is most personal is also most universal."

Over these months I have struggled deeply with the "why" of God's timing of my mother's death. I realized I could not accept what God gives as easily as my mother could in her simple faith and trust. I went through a period of intense anger toward the inscrutable character of God—a natural tendency in the grieving process according to the Old Testament prophets and Psalms.

As I read again in Job 42, I experienced along with Job his response to God in verses 4-6: "You said, 'Listen now, and I will speak; I will question you, and you shall answer me.' My ears had heard of you but now my eyes have seen you. Therefore I despise myself and repent in dust and ashes."

My eyes were opened when I came face-to-face with Christ and His suffering for me. Then I could truly let go and say, "Yes, Lord, after what You suffered for me, this is nothing. I will rejoice in being a partaker of Your suffering!"

> Dear friends, do not be surprised at the painful trial you are suffering, as though something strange were happening to you. But rejoice that you participate in the sufferings of Christ, so that you may be overjoyed when his glory is revealed. (1 Peter 4:12-13)

In *Joy and Strength*, Henry Scott Holland writes:

> It is a tremendous moment when first one is called upon to join the great army of those who suffer. That vast world of love and pain opens suddenly to admit us one by one within its fortress. We are afraid to enter into the land, yet you will, I know, feel how high is the call. It is as a trumpet speaking to us, that cries aloud, "It is your turn—endure. Play your part."

This was my turn. I played my part, but I did not play it well. I can still remember when I almost felt my mother admonishing me for how I was feeling and acting! It was as if she were saying, "Quit acting like such a child. This is part of life. Take what God gives and learn the lessons He wants you to learn."

Forgive me, Lord, for feeling the cost was too great. The cost is nothing compared to Your love for me—You gave Your life. I've only given material things—a dream house, security, stability, time with family, memories. Do with me as You please, for I know Your love transcends anything I can imagine.

The struggle is over. Thank You, Lord, for giving me my turn.

> "[Y]ou will know that I have done nothing . . .
> without cause, declares the Sovereign LORD."
> (Ezekiel 14:23)

Rosalie Flickinger and her husband, Leland, have served at the Black Forest Academy, a school for missionary children, since 1990, as Finance Administrator and chairperson of the Music Department respectively. Leland previously held the position of chairperson of the Music Department at Crown College. Mission work for the Flickingers is a second career.

Who's the Child?

taken from
It's a Wonderful (Mid)Life!

by Sheila Rabe

I was headed to Bible study with my favorite neighbor (who just happens to be my mom), and she was driving. Mom, who has shrunk over the years, sat on a pillow so she could see over the steering wheel. This made her just able to reach the gas pedal with her toes, which—incidentally—are full of lead. (I thought people were supposed to drive slowly when they got old, but I guess no one explained this to Mom.)

We had come down the hill to the highway and were going to make a left-hand turn at one of the rare traffic lights that doesn't have a green turning arrow. The light turned green. Mom started to crank the steering wheel and turn left—into the path of an oncoming truck.

Adrenaline shot out in all directions of my body, screaming, "We're all gonna die!"

"Not yet, Mom," I said, trying to stay calm.

She put on the brakes, let the nice man drive past, then tried again. Another car was coming. "Mom, we have to yield," I said, wondering if I was too young to start wearing Depends.

Mom obligingly braked, then repeated the whole process once more. I guess she figured that the third time's the charm. "Mom, wait!" I shrieked as a red car squeezed past us by half an inch.

The next car, probably fearing for his life, decided to turn left. So Mom cranked the wheel, stomped on the gas with her little lead toes, and we whipped through the signal. The adrenaline in my body returned to its cage, and my heart settled into a normal rhythm. I smiled sweetly at my mother and vowed to do all I could to end her driving days.

Driving is a sign of independence. No one likes to give it up, not even my sweet, tiny, eighty-some-thing-year-old mother. But Mom is stoic. So, when my car died and my brother suggested she pass hers on to me, she said, "There comes a time . . ." and surrendered her driving privileges. The fact that she could help her daughter who needed a car eased the transition to passenger. Now she rides shotgun with my brother or me when we run errands. We hit the card store, drugstore and grocery store. My sister-in-law, who is like a second daughter to Mom, delights in taking her to the shopping mall and encouraging her to buy wild outfits. And Mom, who still is able to live on her own, is content.

If this sounds idyllic, that's because it is. But not every parent is like mine. I've heard it said that as we age, our flaws become magnified—which means there is many a cranky, stubborn parent in Hometown, USA, driving his or her offspring crazy. Chances are we'll not only fight the battle of independence with our teens but with our parents.

One friend experienced a very rough year. She watched her mother, insistent on remaining independent, careen from one trouble to the next. After Mom nearly wrapped her car around a tree, daughter decided it was time Mother moved in with her. But Mother got cold feet, leaving her daughter wondering what scrape Mama would fall into next.

No one likes to admit she no longer functions well on her own. No one likes to admit that her body is crumbling or her mental capacities are slipping. And no child likes to see that happen to his or her parents. One of my survey participants talked candidly of how her mother's slow deterioration affected her. "I miss the fun we used to have," she says.

I still remember the first time I saw my mother limp. We were headed for a mother-daughter tea at her church. Mom looked adorable in her suit and high-heeled shoes, but she favored one leg.

"Mom, what's wrong?" I asked.

"Nothing, dear," she said. "My hip just hurts a little."

As the years passed, we went from "hurts a little" to hurts a lot.

"You've got to get hip replacement surgery," nagged her family and friends. One of her brothers really lit into her, and she got madder than I'd ever seen her. "I'm not going to, and that's that," she said. "Who would take care of Father?"

My father's health had never been the greatest. He'd battled a couple of serious problems and had emerged a hypochondriac. Mom was convinced that if she had hip surgery something awful would happen to Dad and she would be incapacitated and unable to help him.

So she refused surgery and suffered restricted mobility. We used to walk together on the beach at our island home. Then she couldn't get down the stairs to the beach, and I walked alone.

Then came my father's death. He was such a part of all our lives. Granted, he often drove us all nuts. He freely dished out unsolicited advice. He always had a to-do list for his sons when they came to visit. But he adored his family. He was a high-energy, life-of-the-party guy who taught his sons how to laugh and play jokes. Now he was only a memory, which brings me to another point made by a survey participant. One of the scariest things about watching our aging parents is this realization: they won't always be there. When our parents have been a big part of our life, it's hard to imagine life without them. Who will pitch in and watch the kids in an emergency? Who will advise me when I have problems with my husband or my children? Who will support me, pray for me? *Who will love me like my mother?* No one but the Lord. (And He'll love me even better.)

There comes a time when a mother relinquishes the role she has played for so many years. Her daughter moves from ingenue to bride, from bride to older woman. And then, one day, mother steps off the stage. Her daughter becomes the family matriarch. She becomes the support to *her* daughter, who naively believes her mom will always be there . . . until it comes time to take the baton from her mother's weak hands and run the distance allotted to her. That's the reality of life. The only way to emotionally survive this unexpect-edly short cycle is to accept it and to make the most of the time we have with our parents.

My life gets busy. Although my mother lives next door, I'll go several days without doing anything with her. Then I'll think, *I may not have her much longer*. Now is the time to remember her. She wants my laughter now, not my tears at her funeral. She wants flowers in a vase, not on her grave. I stop what I'm doing and go next door for a visit.

One survey participant confessed, "I look at my mother and see the specter of me." We fear that we too will one day say foolish things and embarrass our chil-dren; that our memory will fail, and we'll grope for words that once rolled easily off our tongues; that we'll appear in public wearing tennie runners, drooping knee-high nylons and chartreuse shorts. Or maybe our fear runs to something more basic: the fear of death. We see our parents marching that direction and realize that we too are mortal. We are next in line.

I remember my grandmother sitting in the kitchen, deeply sighing and saying, "I just want to go home."

My mother, like all loving daughters who would rather not face the inevitable, said, "Mother, no you don't."

But Grandma did. Her body was wearing out. Her hus-band and dearest, oldest friends were dead, and she was feeling the call of paradise.

My thoughtful participant shared candidly, "I don't look forward to dying," as in "*So why should Mom?*" Frankly, I don't look forward to dying either. I'm not afraid of my body losing function. But I am afraid of the pain I might go through in the transition into eternity. I do see, however, that most people reach a point in life where death looks less and less like an enemy.

The apostle Paul wrote in Second Corinthians 5:4, "For while we are in this tent, we groan and are burdened, because we do not wish to be unclothed but to be clothed with our heavenly dwelling, so that what is mortal may be swallowed up by life." The first man and woman were meant to live forever in the bodies God created for them, but with their fall from grace came sin, disease and sorrow. After eighty or so years, coping with life in a fallen world gets wearing; we get tired of dragging around a rotting tent. If that body is racked with pain, the spirit longs to escape. There's no sting in death, no victory in the grave. The elderly person knows that. "We . . . would prefer to be away from the body and at home with the Lord" (5:8). She thinks about her worn-out body and says, "How can I lose? Take me, Lord."

Once upon a time, I chaperoned a junior high outing that, if it wasn't from hell, it at least was attacked by it. We rode inner tubes down a river. A scary part of our adventure came when we got caught by nasty currents. We had already rescued one teenager who had fallen off her inner tube further back and were determined not to lose any more. I managed to get my three charges safely near the bank, but lost my inner tube in the process. It disappeared, leaving me clinging to the kids' giant inner tube. But the strong current pulled me away, and I went bobbing off at what felt like fifty miles an hour.

The water was cold, the current was fast, and I had no control over what was happening. My mind said, "Give in. You're going to drown. Relax and let it happen." My body said, "What a good idea!" Just as I went slack, our youth leader got to me and hauled me out.

The mental battle I experienced during my dunking in the river gave me a peek into my future. I know a time will come when, groaning under the weight of a fraying tent, my spirit will say, "Let go. You no longer need this; there is something better ahead."

I already have days when I just don't want to get up, and once up, hear protests from stiff and sore muscles. Some days it is too much trouble to fix my face and hair. (I never had a day like that when I was twenty!) If I have days like this when I'm middle-aged, how will I feel when I'm seventy-five or eighty?

No wonder so many old people sigh and say, "I just want to go home." Home means no more aches and pains, no more suffering, no more tears. Our elderly parents, so burdened with sickness and weak bodies, long to see their parents and mates once more. They long for home. It is hard for us who love them to hear them talk that way, but it's not unnatural for them to do so.

You might have a parent who is still perfectly happy with her tent; she is blithely unaware that her tent is unraveling. She may not remember how to boil water, but she insists on trying to live independently. She expects her children to keep her house in repair, mow her lawn and take her for a ride every Sunday. Or, like my friend, you could have a parent who excels at playing pin the fender on the tree.

If you are part of the "sandwich generation"—stuck between teenagers and aging parents—you probably find it difficult to help both ends of the sandwich. You may even consider running away. You wonder, *When do I get to rest?* You get to rest when you are no longer the sandwich meat, but a slice of bread. Meanwhile, try to build some personal health days into your schedule. Take an afternoon and go to a ball game with your husband. Hop in the car and hit some garage sales. Work out at the gym. Take a sauna, get a massage, do lunch with a friend.

In addition to getting away once in a while, get help. Set aside a quarterly work day when the extended family pitches in to help mom. This takes care of a lot of the painting and patching that needs to be done. Enlist the grandkids' help. Mowing the lawn once a week will teach unselfishness and the importance of caring for our elderly. It will also help keep a close relationship between grandparent and grandchild. If you live out of state, you may have to pay someone to take care of maintenance jobs.

You cannot shrug off a parent's needs, saying, "Someone will take care of Mom." *Someone is* supposed to take care of Mom, and that someone is you. God set this precedent when He told the nation of Israel in Exodus 20:12 to "Honor your father and mother, so that you may live long in the land the LORD your God is giving you." In Matthew 15:3-6, Jesus got after the religious leaders of the day. He bluntly pointed out their hypocrisy when they tried to wiggle out of caring for their aging parents. They said, "I'm afraid I can't spare money for you, folks. I'm already giving to the church" (the equivalent of "I gave at the office"). The apostle Paul summed it up when he instructed Christians to put their religion into practice by caring for elderly members of their family (see 1 Timothy 5:4). This is how we pay back those who sacrificed for us. Just to make sure we get the point, he added, "If anyone does not provide for his relatives, and especially his immediate family, he has denied the faith and is worse than an unbeliever" (5:8).

You may be thinking, *My parents didn't sacrifice for me, I owe them nothing.* One of my survey participants wrote frankly of her neglectful parents, "They both deserve slow, painful deaths." Maybe so. But caring for them anyway may be the most powerful witness of God's power that they will ever see. It demonstrates the love of God in a way words alone can never do.

Sometimes it would just be easier to make Mom move in with us. But we can't always do what is easiest for ourselves, because that might not be best for her. Mom will only go for that kind of arrangement if she feels needed. If she thinks you see her as another child who needs care, she'll die of malnutrition or a broken leg before she gives up her independence.

I have a friend who is determined to move her mother across the country to live with her. Mama's physical health isn't wonderful, and her bank account doesn't look too strong. But she resists all her daughter's well-meant attempts to transplant her. Why? Because Mama has a history and a network of friends where she lives. And although she might complain about finances, she doesn't want her daughter swooping into town and carrying her off. While Mama would appreciate financial help, she doesn't want her whole life tipped upside down.

Funny how that works. Every adult wants to be treated like an adult, no matter how needy she is. Managing this can become extremely challenging as our parents become more childlike and fearful.

Many of my survey participants talked about this issue. When her father needed a serious operation, one woman found her mother harder to deal with. During this time of crisis, her mother became discouraged and negative. The daughter tried to point out the rainbows in the dark clouds over Mama's head, which quickly became draining. Daughter coped by slipping away to take a solitary walk or a bike ride. Those spots of enjoyment helped recharge her batteries so she could return to her mother's side with a positive attitude.

One friend talked about arriving to take Mama to the airport. Mama was ready to go—along with several plastic bags of clothes.

"Those are my clothes for the trip," said Mama.

"Mom, you can't take things in a bag on an airplane. Where's your big suitcase?"

"I don't have a big suitcase."

"Yes, you do," said daughter. She found the suitcase and packed the clothes. Daughter also asked airline personnel to make sure Mama got to her destination. Good idea—because Mama took off in the wrong direction as she left the plane. Several frantic flight attendants chased her down and got her turned around.

One survey participant says she needs to be very specific with her mother. In the past, daughter and family came to visit "sometime in the afternoon." Now Mama wants to know exactly when. Another friend says that if she tells her mother about an outing too far in advance, Mama stews and frets over a million details. If Mama gets short notice, she has less time to worry herself sick.

To help you cope, here is a parent care survival plan to stick on your fridge:

1. When helping my parent gets stressful and I need someone to pray with me, I can call:

2. When I need an emotional break, I will:

3. These Scripture verses help me serve and honor my parent, even when I don't want to:

4. Phone numbers and information I need at my finger-tips:

* * * *

When I volunteered in a nursing home, I saw many aged people who had been planted and then abandoned to thrive as best they could. When I think about them, I wonder if Galatians 6:7—"A man reaps what he sows"—applies to their children. The golden rule certainly does: "Do to others as you would have them do to you" (Luke 6:31). Would I want to be forgotten in my old age? Nope. Does my mother want to be ignored? Definitely not.

Remember, this too shall pass. You didn't remain a child forever. Neither will your mother and father—simply because they won't remain forever. Whether they live in a nursing home or your home, they want and need your respect, love and attention. Our parents cared for us; we can do no less for them. Even if their care was lacking, we still can do no less. Because in caring for others, we honor God.

The Way of a Widow

taken from
A Time for Mercy

by Marie Ens

I was on unfamiliar paths, walking the way of a widow. Daily I searched God's Word, eagerly noting every reference to God's attitude and provision for widows. What I found always brought comfort and confidence.

God is a Father to the fatherless and a Judge who will decide fairly in our behalf.

God used us as an illustration telling the story of a widow who pleaded with a wicked judge who finally gave in to her pleadings. Jesus assured me that, unlike this wicked man, He would certainly respond promptly to my cry. How I cried out to Him! God would not condone anyone taking advantage of us. "Do not take advantage of a widow or an orphan," He commanded, adding, "If you do and they cry out to me, I will certainly hear their cry" (Exodus 22:22-23). I grasped the promise and held it firmly. *God establishes the boundaries of the widow.*

I believed that no one could take away what God decided belonged to me. Jesus spat out His contempt for those who "devoured widows' houses," using this sin to illustrate what despicable sinners the Pharisees were in His eyes. How compassionate He is toward us!

The widow of Nain did not even ask for His help, yet He spied her weeping over her only son and restored him to life. I knew that He saw my tears and understood my needs and would reach out to help me even before I had a chance to ask.

The early church had a list of widows. When these women reached the age of sixty, the church leaders were instructed to care for them. I understood that I was not to go at it alone and that God wanted my physical and temporal needs met.

God would accept my love gifts no matter how small when they showed my dependence on Him. So the widow's mite would become my might, my strength, as I gave all and depended on Him to care for me. Passing over others richer and more powerful, He would use me in His service taking my little "all" and multiplying it. He had done just that for the widow at Zarephath whom He chose to keep His servant Elijah alive during a great famine (1 Kings 17).

How comforting to know that my heavenly Father was aware of my vulnerability, aware that a Christian woman who had sought to be obedient to His command and find shelter in her husband's leadership would be left feeling unprotected when He removed that shelter.

The basis for my requests to my Lord often was simply, "I am one of Your widows." I saw myself as totally dependent on His loving provision for me. How easy then to see myself as weak, timid and fearful. I was soon to learn a lesson about those very things.

One July morning, He began to show me another aspect of what He would do for this widow who depended solely on His might. "He makes my feet like the feet of a deer; he enables me to stand on the heights" (2 Samuel 22:34), I read. The Holy Spirit prompted me to realize that this promise was for *me*, for *now*. He confirmed it as I attended the International Christian Fellowship service and heard the same verse read. Over and over God spoke it to my heart.

"Thank You, . . . but what does it mean?" I asked my Lord.

As I meditated on this truth He began to give me insights. Eagerly I recorded them in my journal. "Sure-footed, confident, daring, able to judge danger, able to bound away, able to see from afar," I wrote one day.

During the next months I found this same verse repeated again and again. Always I sensed that there was still more to understand.

"What else does it mean, Lord?" I begged. I continued to write the insights in my journal. "The mountain goat is up there alone. No one is watching what he does to praise Him," I entered one day. Another day I wrote an observation, drawing a smiley face beside it, "The mountain goat is thinking 'lofty thoughts'!" After a conversation with a friend from Switzerland, I recorded her insights concerning these amazing animals, noting that "when they come to the end of the path and can go no further, they easily leap to another path. When their nourishment is all covered in ice and snow, they use their feet to dig for it. They don't always travel alone; sometimes they are in groups. They can smell danger and they warn one another when it is near. They are very clever, knowing where danger lies and learning to avoid it."

Thousands of miles away in England lived a correspondent who had prayed for me and for Cambodians for many years. My only contact with Tina Milne was through letters. Often she sent just a short note on a postcard.

Five months after God began telling me He would make my feet like the feet of a deer and enable me to go on the heights, I was again the recipient of a postcard from her. She knew nothing of what the Lord had been saying to me. Surely she had the option of choosing from thousands of postcards. Surely there were thousands of promises she could have sent me. But she sent me this one, "He makes my feet like the feet of a deer. He enables me to stand on the heights." The picture on the postcard was breathtaking. I felt like God was saying to me, "You keep asking Me what it means. Let Me show you a picture."

There, high up on a steep, rugged, snowy mountain slope stood one solitary, strong, courageous mountain goat. Its feet were firm and sure on the slippery pathway. It lifted its head and surveyed the barren beauty below. It was obviously confident and unafraid.

"Oh Lord," I breathed in awe, "is that how You see me?"

By His grace, the tentative way of the widow—any widow, including me—leads to heights reached on feet like the feet of a deer.

Monster from the Deep

taken from
In Peril on the Sea

by Robert Bell
and Bruce Lockerbie

Kapitänleutnant Friedrich Markworth, commanding officer of *U-66*, stepped back from the periscope and clapped his hands.

"Direct hits!" Markworth shouted into the speaking tube connected to the control room below the conning tower. "Two of them! She won't last five minutes!"

The chief engineer climbed the ladder to peer into the periscope lens for himself.

"She's keeled over already, Captain. Imagine, less than two minutes! That may be a new record!"

"Do we have identity?" Markworth inquired.

"I'll find out," said the engineer as he slid down the ladder.

It was hardly a room, more like a cubicle curtained off from the rest of the submarine to give the radio operator some quiet in which to concentrate. The operator waved the crewman into silence before he could speak.

Then the radioman removed the headset, stood up and stretched.

"Nothing," he said in reply to the crewman's unspoken question. "I have no information whatever. The ship's radio never put out a message. It must have been knocked out by the first strike. Tell Captain Markworth that I know nothing at all about the ship."

The crewman returned to the control room with the message.

"Take us to the top," the commander told the engineer. "Let's see for ourselves."

The German submarine known as *U-66* was typical of the boats in action throughout World War II. It had been sent with others to harass shipping along the east coast of the United States of America.

Throughout the fall of 1941, Admiral Karl Dönitz had been trying to persuade Adolf Hitler to launch attacks against America's vulnerable east coast. But for reasons of his own, Hitler had rejected Dönitz's argument. Even as late as December 6, the day before Japan's attack on Pearl Harbor, Hitler was still hoping to keep the Americans out of the war. But on December 11, Germany joined Japan in making war on the United States and the American coastline became a German target. Almost immediately, Dönitz sent word to his Submarine Service to head westward toward the sitting ducks in American harbors.

Markworth's first patrol, the *U-66's* sixth mission, left France on June 26 of 1942. By the close of August 30, the day on which this story begins, Markworth had sunk seven ships and damaged several others. An amateur photographer, he sometimes took home movies of the havoc he had created, standing in the tower of his boat and panning the scene of destruction and death with his camera.

The next attack is recorded in *U-66's* official log using Middle European Time, a five-hour difference. Here, in Atlantic time, it reads:

Day: 30 August 1942

7:00 a.m. Rainy, varying visibility. Just went 184 sea miles above water, 1.8 miles under water . . .

10:00 a.m. Smoke in view. Proceeding at top speed.

12:00 p.m. Smoke in sight.

1:08 p.m. Dived.

1:15 p.m. At battle stations.

At the position of 10° 30' north and 55° 34' west, just after Sunday dinner had been served on board the *West Lashaway*, Markworth gave the command. The *West Lashaway* was doomed. The remaining pertinent log entries read:

2:31 p.m. Two individual torpedoes, tubes I and III. Two hits. Strong white explosion. Ship apparently loaded with phosphates.

2:36 p.m. Surfaced.

2:45 p.m. Steamer sunk. Now going at 180° on new course.

4:20 p.m. Wireless message to BDU: Just sunk steamer 4,500 BRT.

269

Lieutenant Donald Gay, commander of the United States Navy Patrol Squadron 31, Trinidad Detachment, flew his PBY over the sun-blanched western Atlantic. To his right lay the coast of South America, 250 miles away; to the left, his partner, Lieutenant Tom Evert, U.S. Navy, patrol plane commander of another PBY. Their mission on this Sunday afternoon: to search for enemy submarines and destroy them. Their special object: to hunt down the deadly *U-66*.

Gay and Evert knew where to look for *U-66*. From reports of yesterday's and today's sinkings they had evidence that the submarine was preying on ships in the latitudes 10° above the equator, just west of the fiftieth meridian. Flying in a half-vee formation, then breaking off from each other for a roll right or left to scan a zone of water, then reforming within hearing distance of each other, the two pilots and friends kept to their course.

Suddenly Donald Gay saw a blip on his radar screen. At the same instant Tom Evert also reacted to what his radar scope showed him. Together the two PBYs rushed toward their target—each other's plane! Fortunately, they realized their mistake just in time to avert a collision and sped past each other, their wings overlapping.

"Any more word about *U-66*?" Gay asked once he had recovered control of his plane.

"No, sir. Seems pretty quiet out there since this morning. Maybe Jerry's doing a little sunbathing this afternoon."

"That'll be the day!" retorted the commanding officer. "Admiral Dönitz doesn't sunbathe and neither do his U-boats. They're all out there someplace just biding their time. We'd better get them before they get any more of us!"

Back at base, Donald Gay looked around the wardroom. "Who's up?" he asked.

"We are, Skipper," said Lieutenant Jack Hillman, motioning to Lieutenant Raymond North. They strode out on the tarmac to the waiting planes to resume the hunt.

At the first sound of the alarm, Robert Bell and Richard Shaw bolted from the crew's quarters and up a short ladder to their cabins. They hadn't heard the watchman's cry, yet without a word between them or from the crews, each somehow knew that this was more than just another regular drill. Before Robert had reached his cabin, the first shuddering blow of a torpedo struck the *West Lashaway* on its starboard side.

The Bells' cabin was portside, opposite the torpedo's wound in the ship's hull. The cabin door had been blown open. Inside Robert found his mother hurrying to put on her dress, his sister fumbling with the cork life jacket.

"Hurry, children," Ethel Bell* said. "Calmly now, but hurry."

Robert helped Mary fasten her jacket and was starting to put on his own when the second strike came with devastating force. Where the first hit had been only damaging, this

---

* *Ethel Bell, a widow, was a missionary in Africa. Because of the war, she and her two children, Robert and Mary, were ordered to return to America. (Her husband, George, had died in a bus accident on an earlier furlough.)*

second thrust was mortal, exploding the fuel bunkers, boilers and cargo bays in a spume of fire and steam, oil and latex. Not more than ten seconds had separated the two direct hits. Immediately the *West Lashaway* began listing to starboard.

The children and their mother froze in panic. Their bunks had collapsed, the light fixture had fallen from the ceiling, the floor seemed to be sliding out from under them. In that moment of stark terror, Ethel Bell called out, "Oh God, help us!" Then, grabbing the children's hands in hers, she led them out of the cabin and up a crazy ladder to the chaos on deck. In their rush they left behind their ditty bags and valuables.

Evidence of disaster spilled out everywhere. Beyond the shattered starboard rail, the waterline was rising rapidly. The starboard lifeboats, to which the Bell family had been assigned, had been dissolved by the second torpedo's blast. Ethel Bell and her children were directed across the treacherously sloping deck to the portside boats, tilting steeply as the crippled ship began to slide over on its side.

The Bells clambered into a boat, but no sooner had they entered it than the officer in charge shouted at them, "Get out! Get out!" The ship was now listing so severely that these boats had been forced immovably against their davits. There was no way for them to be lowered. Mrs. Bell and Mary jumped from the boat into the water, but Robert's feet were caught under him. While he struggled to free himself, the entire ship slid beneath the surface. From first alert to the ship's sinking had been less than two minutes.

Suddenly Robert became aware that he was no longer sinking. There was light—and air! But Robert could not see. His eyes were glued shut by the globs of palm oil and other spillage through which he had emerged. The residue of lost cargo coated his hair and face like a mask. Sputtering, coughing and gagging—his head barely above the swell—Robert could hear the sound of voices, hushed tones, no longer screaming or shouting. Then gradually, through his still-blurred eyes, he began to distinguish objects in the water—bits of planking, articles of clothing, and other forms and shapes too terrible to identify.

"Mother! Mary!" he called out.

Mary answered from close by. Then his mother spoke, some sixty yards away. "Children, over here. Oh, thank You, Lord!"

Together Mary and Robert swam to where their mother was holding on to a plank. Moments before, they had been enjoying their voyage home. Now they were clinging to life, their immediate security only a shattered strip of lumber.

As Robert held on to the floating wood, his eyes gradually lost their blurriness and he saw the two other pairs of hands gripping the plank. On the ring finger of his mother's left hand, he caught sight of her wedding band.

"Well, Mother," he gulped between the swell of the waves, "at least you still have your wedding ring!"

Hope and help were also at hand. Around the perimeter of the oil slick the Bells could discern four wooden rafts. In addition to its lifeboats, the *West Lashaway*, like every other ship, had carried four rafts mounted on steeply angled skids so as to slide easily into the water.

Ordinarily, a loosened line would have released each raft. But when the second torpedo ripped into the ship, the rafts were blown overboard like chips of wood. These floating crates, borne up by the watertight drums, weighed almost half a ton each, yet so great was the torpedo's explosion that these boxes had been catapulted from their moorings like rockets.

Other survivors had crawled up out of the water and onto the rafts. Even now the Bells could see people being hauled aboard these bobbing bits of flotsam.

"Over here! Three more over here!" the Bells called.

While they waited for rescue, a strange humming sound filled their clogged ears. Then, as if from a scene in a monster movie, an unthinkable shape from the depths broke the water's plane. Less than fifty yards from where the Bells hung on to their plank, the German U-boat appeared. Its gray-streaked tower proudly bore its insignia, the head of a snarling lion with fangs threatening.

Paralyzed with terror, Robert could hear the metallic grating as the hatch opened and four uniformed officers appeared inside the tower. One of them, bearded and laughing as he spoke, gave orders to the other three. He seemed to be looking directly at the Bells.

Now, for sure we will die, Robert thought. His fear was confirmed in the next instant when the Germans let go with a round of rapid fire from an automatic weapon. Instinctively, Robert ducked below the slime of oil and latex. The firing continued for several more rounds while Robert waited for the bullets to strike him.

But nothing happened and the boy soon resurfaced. Apparently the Germans were firing aimlessly, not shooting at anyone or anything, merely testing the working condition of their weapons in case they should be needed.

A few minutes later, the men crawled back down the hatch, leaving their victims with neither threats nor offers of assistance. Like other soldiers and sailors, they simply took no notice of the human consequences of war. The humming of the submarine's diesel engines began reverberating at a higher pitch. Slowly the hull evaporated, the deck with its cannons and, finally, the tower disappeared from view, leaving no trace that *U-66* had ever been there.

Once again the sea was calm.

Klaus Herbig, the youngest officer, closed the hatch of *U-66* and slid to the control room floor as the boat submerged.

"Did you get the ship's name, Herbig?" asked the sub's commander.

"No, Captain," Herbig replied.

"You are sure?"

"Yes, sir."

"Too bad. Herbig, tell Degener-Böning so that he can keep his records properly."

Friedrich Markworth paced in the little area dominated by the tower instruments.

"Now, what do you suppose that ship was doing in these parts? She's too small for a tanker. She's just a little steamer that strayed into dangerous waters."

Markworth laughed again. "And what do you suppose our little friend was carrying in her belly?"

"Whatever it was, sir," someone said, "it's no good to anybody now."

"Yes, but what an explosion!" added another. "It was like a pickle factory going off. Did you see that slime all over the water? Poor wretches trying to survive that mess would be better off dead."

"Best not to think about them," the commander cautioned. "We are at war. They are at risk on the high seas. It is all fate. What's more, you'll never see any of them again."

The submarine commander turned and began walking toward the ladder, then stopped abruptly.

"And Herbig, don't forget to ask Degener-Böning if the ship got off any final radio message. I'd like to know whether or not we should expect company later this evening."

Once more the handsome Markworth laughed. It had been a long day with much excitment. Two sinkings within ten hours of each other. Surely Dönitz would be informed soon. How proud he would be of his former cadet! Perhaps, with just a little luck, there might be an honor in store. After all, his predecessor Zapp had won the Knight's Cross.

Markworth fingered the collar of his shirt, feeling for the medal that would someday be there. Enough for one day. Tomorrow there would be more Allied ships to sink.

Kapitänleutenant Friedrich Markworth eased himself onto his bunk and slept soundly.

Robert Bell is the son of Ethel Bell, who with his sister, Mary, and mother, survived the experiences chronicled in *In Peril on the Sea*.

Bruce Lockerbie has served as the Dean of Faculty at Stony Brook School in Stony Brook, New York. He is currently the chairman of Paideia, Inc.

Grandmothering: The Great Frontier

taken from
It's a Wonderful (Mid)life!

by Sheila Rabe

May you live to see your children's children. (Psalm 128:6)

These days, I kiss my son on the cheek at the risk of getting whisker burn. He is big and manly—and not ashamed to hug his mother. But the only person he cuddles with now is his girlfriend. Even if he were willing, I wouldn't risk him sitting on my lap. He would squish me. My daughter, Honey, has always been affectionate, but she has finally taken my advice to get a life. She is never home. So I have no one to nurture but the cat. (Well, the rat too, but I am not that desperate!)

This, I have concluded, is why we need grandchildren.

Grandmotherhood is the step after motherhood for many of us. And, like motherhood, it comes with its own set of job requirements. I am not yet there, so I asked several experts (real-life grandmothers) for their opinions on the fine art of grandmothering.

They agreed that being a grandmother gives double the pleasure. You can enjoy your offspring's children—and give them back before the thrill wears off. Here is how the grandmothers I talked to defined themselves:

Grandmothers are usually happy and cuddly

A lot of kids like to hug their grandmas, and grandmas like to hug their grandchildren. A child happily anticipates going to Grandma's house. In a child's mind, "Grandma" equals warmth, security and deep contentment.

Grandmothers are not as strict as mothers

The grandmas I talked to do not run houses with no rules, but they do have fewer rules.

One grandmother related that after a visit to her house, her grandson left his clothes in a heap on his bedroom floor. "Pick up your clothes," said Mom.

"I don't have to pick them up at Grandma's," replied her son.

I'll bet you can guess what his mother's reply was, and yes, he did pick up his clothes.

At Grandma's house you may not have to clean your room, or your place, or worry about spoiling your appetite with a late afternoon candy bar.

Grandmothers listen

They don't usurp a mother's position, but they want to listen to a grandchild's troubles and offer advice if asked. Many times Honey hiked up the road to Grandma's house to pour out her troubles when things weren't going well at school or she and Mom had fought.

Grandmothers keep confidences

My mother, I'm sure, has heard some interesting tales. I know that if a child confided a drug or other serious problem to her, she would have no compunction about turning stool pigeon. But for the less serious secrets she proved herself a safe repository to two generations of grandchildren.

Grandmothers take time

Everyone else is busy trying to earn a living, clean the house and get to softball practice, soccer practice or music lessons. Grandmothers may be the last line of defense against the child-gobbling whirlpool of busyness. Grandma takes time to sit with her grandchild in a big, stuffed armchair to read a story. Grandma shows you how to roll out a pie crust or takes you on a walk to collect autumn leaves.

Grandma isn't trying to make payments on a house and a minivan. She understands the value of slowing down and taking time to enjoy life. And if another human being understands enjoying life, it's a child. That makes grandchild and grandparent a perfect match!

Here are tips I gleaned on how to be a good grandmother. (If you are already doing them, congratulations! You earn a grandmothering gold medal.)

Leave the door open a crack

Any bedroom can be a scary place at night when you're small. My son tells me now that he was terrified to sleep in my old bedroom at Grandma's house because of a stuffed owl she stored there. That thing came to life every time we went to visit Grandma, and he was never quite able to explain to Grandpa why he kept creeping down the stairs to the safety of the light and the grown-ups. Maybe that was because Grandpa kept chasing him back up the stairs, growling, "Get in bed!"

Always have popsicles

Grandma's house has treats, great smells and fun times. For kids, great times don't have to cost a lot. A popsicle is hot stuff when you're five.

Smile at dirty clothes

You can do that now, you know. You don't have to fuss and worry about Suzie's new outfit. You didn't buy it—and you've learned that Suzie is more important than the clothes she's wearing.

Relax and enjoy

Now that you have time, you can do outings with the grandkids that you always wanted to do with the kids: lunch out at a fancy tearoom, a trip to the art museum, hide-and-seek in the backyard.

When I see a harried mother snapping at her children, I want to put my arm around her and say, "Please don't. You'll look back someday, relive every harsh word you uttered and be so sorry. You are the sun these little ones revolve around, and your approval means so much. Those older women who said they grow up so fast were right. Love these little ones now while you have the chance."

So far, I haven't done this. I'm a gutless coward and don't want to get punched in the nose. But I am going to work up my nerve one of these days and do it.

Were you one of those harried, snappish moms? You don't have to hurry now, and you don't have to snap. You can meander down the river of life and allow your grandchildren to bob along in your gentle wake. In this crazy world, you may be their only peaceful harbor.

Spoil 'em and send 'em home

Children need someone who will give them a second helping of pie or let them stay up past their bedtime. Do it. Walk on the edge. When the kids have worn you out, you can wave good-bye, kick off your shoes and collapse on the couch with a cup of tea.

Not every grandmother can send her grandkids home these days. In some cases, grandma's house *is* home. The '60s produced more than hippies and tie-dyed clothes. It produced irresponsible parents who would rather run after a good time than care for their offspring. Often the grandparents step in and start child-rearing all over again. I salute those of you who have shouldered that responsibility. God grant you wisdom and strength.

And He will. He gave Sarah strength to become a mother at ninety. He will give you strength to raise a child, whatever your age.

Participate

The saddest thing I ever heard were the words of a friend's mother. Upon hearing that her daughter was pregnant, she said: "Don't expect me to baby-sit." *Why*

283

not? I ask. We are not turtles who hatch our young and then swim off. (It is turtles that do that, isn't it?) We are part of the cycle of life, and if we are part of the body of Christ, God expects us to support the next generation.

This is not to say that you have to do your children's job for them. Maybe your son or daughter is pursuing the "American dream": huge house, three-car garage with three cars in it, the latest in television, computers, cell phones—and the yearly vacation in Hawaii. If so, you don't need to support his or her habit by turning your house into Grandma's Day Care. (Unless you think that someone must be there for the kids—and that someone is Grandma. And you could have a valid point there.) But if your grandchildren's parents live modestly, try to serve God and raise a godly family, then certainly do all you can to help. Helping is the action that distinguishes a noble character. And the woman who says, "Don't expect me to baby-sit," needs to have her tongue taken away and not given back until she learns how to use it more wisely.

Many of us live too far away to be as actively involved with our children as we would like. For those of us separated by distance, thankfully we live in a high-tech age. E-mail, telephones, tape recorders and video cameras help us stay in touch. Grandmother Joan Treary has hooked up a camera to her computer, which allows her to do conference calls. She is also a firm believer in sending goody boxes to the grandchildren at holidays. A box of stuffed bunnies and candy at Easter reminds children that they have grandparents who love them, and it certainly encourages them to associate Grandma with good things. . . .

If you are skilled in crafts or sewing, make keepsakes for your grandchildren to treasure. I have one of my mother's delicate, handmade garters stored in my hope chest for the day that Honey decides to get married. If Grandma doesn't last that long, her granddaughter will have something special made with love for her by Grandma.

You don't have to make garters or embroider fancy pillowcases. A handmade sock puppet with button eyes can be a real treasure to a child. So can a drawing or a poem written especially for him or her. One grandmother I know enjoys sewing dresses for her granddaughters. I suspect those granddaughters take the beautiful dresses for granted. A day will come, though, when they will realize how special those dresses were. They'll feel specially loved.

Psalm 127:3-5 tells us that children are a blessing from the Lord. That's true. And grandchildren are a double blessing. If you don't appreciate your blessing the first time around, grandchildren give you a second chance.

Chivalry—
The Lost Virtue

taken from
*Out of the Locker Room
of the Male Soul*

*by Steve Masterson
with George McPeek*

O ur sons rarely see us practice the lost virtue of
chivalry with our wives, our daughters and with
other women in everyday life. A prime example
of what we have lost as a society is powerfully portrayed
in an incident that took place during the sinking of the
Titanic. According to an article in *Reader's Digest*, when
the ship hit an iceberg and sank, only about one-third of
the passengers survived, and most of these were
women and children. Later, a surviving ship's officer
was asked why. He replied that "women and children
first" was the law of human nature. Apparently, many
male passengers refused to enter lifeboats until they
were sure all the women and children were safe.[1]

It's a strange paradox that we have put women on the
Supreme Court and in corporate chairs of executive
power, made them judges, politicians and police-
women, all the while stripping them of the freedom to
walk our streets in both city and country in physical and

relational safety. This erosion of civility is due in part to feminists who saw chivalry as another form of male domination dressed in white gloves.

But the bottom line has more to do with the breakdown of authority structures where restraint, sacrifice, duty, self-control and self-discipline have all gone the way of chivalry. As life is cheapened by rampant pornography that degrades and subjects women to being sex objects for male sensual gratification, and by abortion that destroys the baby's right to live, we realize an even more serious area of protection is gone.

When manners and etiquette were a part of life, a certain degree of self-restraint was evident in homes, schools and churches. These restraints came to shield women and provide them with a sense of security. Men, it's time for a revival of old-fashioned restraint. Chivalry as a virtue and safety net has been replaced with a form of cultural anarchy that encourages immediate gratification and maximum self-expression, whatever the price. My sense is that women would welcome a little old-fashioned chivalry and restraint.

In the past, chivalry formed an additional element of control, over and above the law, which enabled society to protect itself against offenses which the law could not touch. This virtue of chivalry, like a code of manners, was far more effective than today's politically correct movement with its speech police and hateful speech laws.

Fathers, when we relearn and model respect for women and the self-restraint it implies, violence against women will decline in everyday life. Our sons and young men will begin to see how honor is given to women in practical ways. Incivility is a form of sexual harassment against women that is today a symptom of a far deeper cheapening of life. Older men, teach the younger men self-restraint by practicing some good old-fashioned chivalry with your spouse, your daughters and with older and younger women in your world.

Dad, Daughter and Dating

I will never forget our oldest daughter's first date. As the young man came to pick her up at our house, I stood—with the other four family members—behind the dining room curtains and sneaked a look to see if he would see her to her side of the car and open the door for her. I had told my three daughters that if the young men who came to date them did not pass their first test—opening the door of the car to seat them—they were history. The whole family held its breath. He did it. He passed! He is now her husband and our son-in-law! We love him and so does our daughter.

You see, my three daughters and one son see me open doors for their mother, help her on with her coat, walk on the street side of the sidewalk, carry heavy grocery bags for her, wash the kitchen floor, vacuum the house. Our three daughters have grown up to expect men to treat them this way. Our son will hopefully repeat what he sees his father practice—chivalry, respect and self-restraint, all of which protect a woman's sense of honor and femininity. Come on, men, let's do it, and make our homes, churches, communities and workplaces a safe haven for women!

One other area that desperately needs teaching and modeling is spiritual chivalry. Spiritual chivalry is when we as fathers personally and publicly model being keepers of the Scriptures, defenders of the faith, protectors of the poor and pursuers of justice. Our sons need to see us personally reading the Word, praying and living by the commandments of God in our homes. They need to experience us reading the Word and praying together with them and with the whole family. They need to experience us challenging them when they are out of line with scriptural truth. We need to be passionate defenders of the church, loyal and involved.

Incarnating the Word of God and the Spirit of God to our sons, our families and to the world around us is an important form of spiritual chivalry that will set us apart as men after the heart of God.

One winter morning several years ago around 6:30 a.m., our son Scott came into the living room dragging his portable hand-controlled hockey game. I was in the midst of my personal devotions.

"Daddy, Daddy," he said, "can you play hockey with me?"

"Not right now, son," I said. "When I'm done spending this time worshiping God, then I will have a game with you before you go to school."

He went off to play in another room. Fifteen minutes later he came back and asked a very profound question for an eight-year-old boy. "Daddy, do you *have* to do that or do you *want* to?"

"Son," I said, "I enjoy doing this with the Lord."

What an opportunity to speak into my son's life, to bless him by living out before him what it means to be a defender of that which is most important in life—to worship and love the Lord my God with all my heart, soul, mind and strength.

Fathers, be spiritually chivalrous before your sons. As they too become defenders of the Word, the faith, the church, the poor, they will also be men who defend and protect life, women and children. Imagine the result—safe fathers, safe sons; safe homes, safe schools; safe churches and safe communities.

Christ has called us to follow in His steps regarding our attitudes and behavior toward women. I encourage all men whose hearts are after God's to hold this aspect of their maleness up to the light of Christ's love and allow God the Father to guide them. Only then can we as men express more of our male potential. Only then can our women live in a community that is truly safe.

Endnote

1. Linda Lichter, "A Little Chivalry Wouldn't Hurt," *Reader's Digest*, Canadian edition (December 1993), 71.

Steve Masterson is a graduate of Prairie Bible Institute, Providence College, Trinity Evangelical Divinity School and Grace Theological Seminary. He is the National Director of Education for PromiseKeepers Canada. Steve and his wife Jackie have four children and live in Manitoba, Canada.

George McPeek is a graduate of Canadian Bible College and Wheaton Graduate School. An ordained minister and long-time missionary to North American Indians, he is the founder of *Indian Life* magazine and has served as Editorial Director at Christian Publications. George and his wife Bessie have three sons.

Make Good Memories Now

taken from the
Personally Yours article
"Make Good Memories Now"

by William R. Goetz

The scenes replay themselves in my mind as I reflect on pages from a family album. "Don't be so stupid!" is the soundtrack from one—a homework session in which my own distaste for math spills over in frustration while helping my son to complete his assignment.

"Hilarious laughter"—boisterous enough to literally cause several family members to roll on the carpet. The scene is from one of the periodic Family Night talent shows which included an imitation of Curious George!

These two memories, from among thousands available, come from the opposite ends of the spectrum of life with a family of five children, now all grown, married and the parents of our twelve grandchildren.

Looking back, contrasting emotions come—regret over the events at the hurtful end of the spectrum, and great joy and deep satisfaction over the activities at the other end of the scale. How can parents avoid those things that scar family relationships, producing damaging effects and unpleasant memories? On the other hand, what can be done to ensure satisfying family life experiences with positive effects and ultimately good memories?

Since children have an amazing ability to grow up quickly and be gone before you know it, it's particularly important for parents of younger children to consider and follow practices that will maximize the good and minimize the bad.

While the following lists are far from exhaustive and I am far from being an expert in family life matters, the do's and don't's listed here have proven helpful in our experience.

1. **DON'T be permissive, neglectful, authoritarian or dictatorial in your parenting style.** Each of these parental styles are an imbalance between love and discipline. *Permissive* parents equate love with giving their children whatever they want without any consistent disci-

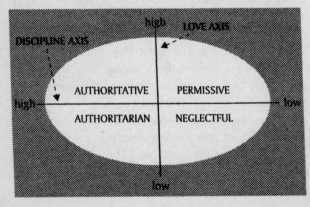

pline or control. *Neglectful* parents give neither love nor direction. *Authoritarian* parents discipline severely without love or warmth, and *dictatorial* styles overlook the input of others—especially teenagers. Studies have revealed that all these styles produce virtually the same results in children—a high rate of failure to accept or follow parental values.

2. **DO be authoritative.** Children need to know they are loved but also that parents are in control and will fairly enforce the prescribed family standards and guidelines.

3. **DON'T fight in front of your kids.** The findings of a ten-year divorce-prevention study reveals that "destructive marital battles lower children's self-esteem, and may act as a time bomb harming the later formation of intimate relationships by them."

4. **DO allow your children to see that disagreements can be settled in a sensible, peaceable fashion.** Demonstrate how to "fight fair."

5. **DON'T put your children down.** To use denigrating terms like "stupid," "clumsy," "dumb" or "ugly" is incredibly harmful and can have lifelong negative effects.

6. **DO encourage and build up your children.** "You're the best," "Good for you," "I love you" and dozens of other encouraging words, honestly uttered, have the power to nourish your child's sense of confidence and worth.

7. **DON'T get so busy that you have no time to communicate with your family.** Career or business success is pretty hollow if one's family is lost in the process.

8. **DO make time to listen and talk, to teach and encourage.** Read together and play games.

9. **DO make time for family fun**. Kite flying, skating, fishing, picnics, a trip to the zoo, shopping, camping—the list of things to do is endless. Fun activities like these provide a foundation for solid relationships that can sustain future shocks. Warm memories of weekly family nights, with their periodic talent shows, still bring smiles to our family members.

10. **DO utilize the concept of a periodic Family Council**. This is a good way to air out and solve problems and to reinforce the principles which govern your family.

11. **DO seek to provide good role-models for your children**. Don't expect your children to be the kind of person you are not willing to be. That includes doing everything necessary and possible to maintain a two-parent home. Numerous studies make it clear that divorce makes victims of children—even adult children. Girls will be better able to love their own mate if they have had a father who loves their mother and them. And boys learn how to be good husbands from watching their mother and dad in action.

Obviously, the ability to live in love is best realized if both husband and wife have a personal relationship with God. As both grow in their vertical relationship with the Lord Jesus Christ, they will find themselves growing closer to each other in the horizontal relationship.

Such an approach to family life is not easy. It requires lots of hard work, sacrifice and faith. But it's well worth it. You—in cooperation with God—can make it happen.

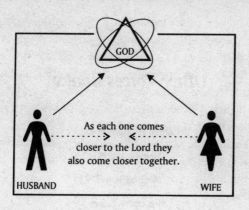

As each one comes
closer to the Lord they
also come closer together.

HUSBAND

WIFE

GOD

William R. Goetz has served in various ministerial capacities—denominational youth coordinator, pastor and vice-president of a publishing house. He is the author of eight books including *Apocalypse Next*, *Once upon an Easter*, *Once upon a Christmas*, *UFOs: Friend, Foe or Fantasy* and *The Economy to Come*.

Other Voices Books

Church-Planting Voices

Healing Voices

Holiness Voices

Missionary Voices

Prayer Voices

Voices on the Glory